CHALLENGING LEVEL

Catching Fire
A Teaching Guide

by Mary Elizabeth

Community Strand

To Mike.

Copyright © 2014 Mary Elizabeth
All rights strictly reserved.

Printed in USA

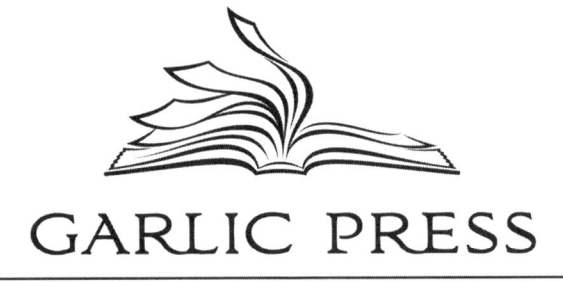

Educational Materials for Teachers and Parents
899 South College Mall Road
Bloomington, IN 47401

www.garlicpress.com

In order to make it easy to use this teaching guide with digital and paperback versions, page numbers from *Catching Fire* for use in locating vocabulary words, quotations, and chapter beginnings match both the Kindle eBook and the Scholastic, Inc. paperback   ISBN -13: 978-0-439-02353-5

Cover Art – Cinna pinning the mockingjay pin on Katniss's scarf at the start of the Victory Tour, p. 41
Chapter Art – President Snow whispering in Katniss's ear that he knows about her kiss with Gale, p. 29
Strategy Page and Writer's Forum Art – Haymitch consoling Katniss on the train for not having control of her own future, p. 45

The purchaser of this book may reproduce any portion hereof, but not substantially the entire book, for classroom or nonprofit organizational use in an amount not to exceed one copy per pupil as an aid to classroom discussion. Copies may be made for not more than one course in the school or organization. Charging for copies or otherwise using the copies for commercial use is strictly prohibited.

Publisher: Douglas M. Rife
Cover and interior illustrator: Ginny Joyner
Interior design: Mary Elizabeth
Cover design: Jenn Taylor

ISBN 978-1-930820-01-2
Order Number GP-206

Table of Contents

Notes to the Teacher	5
The Elements in this Literature Guide	5
Teaching with Digital Editions	7
Introducing the Literature	7
Bibliography	8
Suzanne Collins and the Hunger Games Trilogy	9
The Hunger Games Movies	9
Common Core Correlation	10
• Strategy 1: Beginning the Second Book in a Trilogy	11

Part I "The Spark"

Chapter 1	**Back in District 12**	12
	• Strategy 2: Understanding the Series Reading Process	14
	• Strategy 3: Charting Character Development	16
Chapter 2	**A Visit from the President**	17
	• Strategy 4: Plot—Analyzing the Use of Flashback, Recap, and Foreshadowing	19
	• Strategy 5: Analyzing Choices	20
	• Strategy 6: Analyzing Control of the Setting	22
	• Writer's Forum 1: Translating Fiction into Drama	23
Chapter 3	**The Victory Tour Begins**	24
	• Strategy 7: Challenging the Status Quo	25
Chapter 4	**Choosing Friendship; Arrival in District 11**	27
	• Strategy 8: Predicting and Recognizing Other's Perceptions	29
	• Writer's Forum 2: Comparing/Contrasting Books in a Series	30
Chapter 5	**Peeta Proposes; President Snow Is Not Satisfied**	31
	• Strategy 9: Analyzing Assumptions	33
	• Strategy 10: Identifying Figures of Speech	34
Chapter 6	**The President's Party; Uprising in District 8**	35
	• Strategy 11: Understanding How Symbols and Motifs Are Developed	36
	• Writer's Forum 3: Writing a Short Research Report	37
Chapter 7	**Meeting Gale at the Lake to Plan an Escape**	38
	• Strategy 12: Understanding Complex Motivations	40
Chapter 8	**The Whipping**	41
	• Writer's Form 4: Writing Up an Investigation	42
Chapter 9	**Katniss Plans an Uprising; Second Trip to the Lake**	43
	• Strategy 13: Understanding Parallels and Repetition	45
Test: Chapters 1–9		46

Part II "The Quell"

Chapter 10	**Bonnie and Twill**	47
	• Strategy 14: Understanding Shockers	49
Chapter 11	**The Electrified Fence; The Family Book**	50
Chapter 12	**The Prep Team Arrives: The Quarter Quell Card**	52
	• Strategy 15: Interpreting Intentional Contradictions	53
	• Strategy 16: Considering Possible Consistency Issues	54
Chapter 13	**Katniss and Haymitch Make a Deal; Training; Reaping**	55

Catching Fire: A Teaching Guide   3

Table of Contents, cont.

Chapter 14	**Other Victors; How Haymitch Won the Quell**	57
	• Writer's Forum 5: Writing a Letter of Farewell	59
Chapter 15	**Meeting Victors and Chariot Ride; the New Avox**	60
Chapter 16	**Making Allies/Friends; Time with the Gamemakers**	61
	• Strategy 17: Identifying Tropes—Chekhov's Gun	63
Chapter 17	**The Tributes Take Charge of the Interviews**	64
Chapter 18	**The Mockingjay Dress; Pregnancy; Attack on Cinna**	66
Test: Chapters 10–18		67

Part III "The Enemy"

Chapter 19	**Unexpected Alliance; Peeta Electrocuted**	68
Chapter 20	**Search for Water; Tree Rat and Spile; Tolling Bells**	69
Chapter 21	**Fog and Monkeys; Death of Mags**	70
Chapter 22	**Johanna Joins Alliance with Beetee and Wiress**	71
Chapter 23	**Figuring Out the Clock; Spinning Island**	73
Chapter 24	**Jabberjay Attack; Peeta's Locket**	74
	• Strategy 18: Assessing Various Types of Persuasion	75
Chapter 25	**Beetee's Plan**	76
	• Writer's Forum 6: Writing Instructions or Directions	78
Chapter 26	**Johanna's Attack; Katniss Completes Beetee's Plan**	79
Chapter 27	**Rescue of the Tributes; the Rebellion Begins**	81
	• Strategy 19: Understanding Logical Fallacies and Narrative Misdirection	83
	• Strategy 20: Identifying Themes in a Series	85
	• Writer's Forum 7: Comparing Two Treatments	86
Test: Chapters 19–27		87

Theme Pages
- Odds and Chance — 88
- Debts and Owing — 88
- Appearance vs. Reality — 88
- Competition, Alliance, and Self-Interest — 88
- Abuse — 89
- Morality and Virtue — 89

Answer Pages — 90
  Chapter, Strategy, Writer's Forum, and Test Page Answers in Order — 90
  Theme Page Answers — 111

Notes to the Teacher

The Discovering Literature Series is designed to develop students' appreciation for good literature and to improve reading comprehension. The Challenging Level focuses on reading strategies that help students construct meaning as they read, as well as make connections between and among texts. The strategies taught in each guide reflect the demands of the particular literature selection, and material can be adapted or skipped to suit both class focus and students' developmental level, or even adapted for book club use.

Every teacher of literature faces a quandary in that the experience of literature—suspending one's disbelief and getting lost in the world of a story (aesthetic reading)—and the analysis of literature (efferent reading) are mutually exclusive: it is impossible to engage in both simultaneously. Thus, this guide is designed to be used with at least three different reading modes:

- **Aesthetic/Analytic** Students read the book through first for the experience of the story (with or without vocabulary preparation, depending on the student) and use the guide afterwards to work on comprehension and analysis;
- **Chapter-by-Chapter** Students read after limited preparation (possibly only vocabulary), but a thorough check-in on comprehension and analytic understanding after each chapter ensures comprehension;
- **Guided Reading** Students' reading is scaffolded by, for example, using one or more of the Journal and Discussion Topics to provide a purpose for reading each chapter (being careful to select questions that do not give away major plot elements), and following up as in the other modes.

Readers of the Hunger Games series are likely to be influenced by the movie versions and the accompanying publicity, limiting their ability to imagine the story with the sole influence of Collin's words. If your students are in this situation, it is best to address the influence explicitly, comparing and contrasting the versions.

THE ELEMENTS IN THIS LITERATURE GUIDE

Page Numbers

To make it easier to teach students who have different editions, page numbers that match both paperback and Kindle editions are used to locate vocabulary words, quotations, and chapter beginnings. *HG* and *CF* distinguish the two books.

Chapter Pages

Each Chapter Page is organized into three sections: **Chapter Vocabulary**, **Journal and Discussion Topics**, and a **Chapter Summary**.

The **Chapter Vocabulary** identifies challenging words and provides page numbers and definitions for the specific usage in the book. Introducing the **Chapter Vocabulary** prior to students' reading in any mode can help insure that their reading is not disrupted by unknown words, but since there may be a large amount of unfamiliar vocabulary, you may wish to do this over a period of time, not all at once. More interesting vocabulary activities will be possible if you treat multiple chapters' worth of vocabulary at once, and more meaningful vocabulary exercises will improve retention. A Vocabulary Study feature that includes suggested activities for the vocabulary of the entire trilogy is offered at the end of *Mockingjay: A Teaching Guide*. If you do choose to work by chapter, you could have students:

1. identify relationships between and among words, creating a web or other graphic that shows these relationships and adding related words.
2. keep an eye out for multiple meaning words and synonyms (words that Collins uses in multiple, different meanings are marked "MM" in the vocabulary lists.)

Catching Fire: A Teaching Guide 5

Notes to the Teacher

3. use a set of words in a piece of writing, for example a poem, a personal anecdote, a one-act play, or a journal written in the persona of a character;
4. research the etymology of a set of vocabulary words;
5. make and exchange puzzles made with vocabulary words;
6. write and exchange cloze exercises using the vocabulary words;
7. identify subcategories of vocabulary, for example, words about nature and hunting, verbs, words naming character attributes, six-syllable words, etc.

The **Journal and Discussion Topics** can be used as prompts for entries in students' Reading Response Journals if you choose to use them, as questions for discussion to help students become deeply engaged with the literature, and/or to check comprehension. If you wish to interact with students using their journals, the dialogue will be facilitated if you periodically collect the journals and respond to students' comments. It is important for students to know beforehand whether their journals are private or public. Even if they are public, many educators believe that journals should not be corrected or graded, but only recorded as being used. You may also wish to keep your own journal.

Discussion can take place between partners, in small groups, or as a whole class. Students may also wish to reflect on the discussion in their journals. Discussion starters include:

1. review of predictions made for the chapter and whether they were accurate.
2. group retelling of the chapter in which everyone participates.
3. each group member sharing:
    a. the most striking moment in the chapter for him or her;
    b. a question she or he would like to ask the author or a character; or
    c. what he or she liked most or least about the chapter.
4. analysis of how the chapter relates to the preceding chapters.

The **Chapter Summary** for each chapter is included for teacher use only. While the name I've given to the chapter (Collins does not name her chapters) provides an at-a-glance review of the chapter, the summary has enough details to refresh your memory about specific contents of each chapter. The summaries should never be used to replace reading the work of literature. Note that while the suggested questions always include a summarization idea, these questions are couched so that the summaries provided in this book will not provide adequate answers.

Strategy Pages

Strategy Pages are developed to increase students' understanding of strategies they can use to enhance their understanding of literature. A strategic approach does not eschew teaching skills, but takes instruction farther by helping students understand how and when to deploy their skills, that is, choose appropriate skills to employ in various literary situations. Having a strategic understanding of how meaning is made by the interaction of authors' words and readers' understanding and imagination can lead to enriched reading experiences. Students will have the opportunity to consider topics such as:

- Collins's use of flashback, recap, and foreshadowing
- how Collins uses figurative speech and the trope called Chekhov's Gun
- the identification of continuity errors as opposed to intentional contradictions that further the plot

You may copy and distribute Strategy pages. Students can answer on the back of the page or on a separate sheet of paper. Some Strategy Page questions require ongoing attention as the students continue reading.

Tests

At the end of each of the three parts of the novel, a comprehensive **Test** has been provided for your use. Each test includes vocabulary exercises and short essay topics. You may copy and distribute these pages, which students may complete with or without access to the text, as you decide.

Writer's Forum Pages

Each **Writer's Forum** page presents instruction about a particular genre and directions for a particular writing task in that genre. Assignments draw on both the literature and students' own experience of the text. You can choose from these suggestions or substitute your own creative-writing ideas.

As you plan writing lessons, allow enough time for students to engage in the writing process:

- **Prewrite** (brainstorm and plan their work)
- **Draft** (give a shape to their ideas on paper)
- **Review** (revisit their work with an eye to improving it, on their own as well as with peers, with you, or with other reviewers)
- **Revise** (make changes that they feel will improve their draft)
- **Proofread** (check for accuracy in grammar, mechanics, and spelling)
- **Publish** (present their work to others in some way)

Theme Pages

There are several different ways to approach theme, starting with Strategy Page: Identifying Themes (p. 85) and the Theme Pages (pp. 88–89). You can also set this work in the context of other works of literature that focus on community using our other literature guides in "The Community" series or other works with a community theme, for example, these dystopias:

- *Animal Farm* or *Nineteen Eighty-Four* by George Orwell
- *Brave New World* by Aldous Huxley
- *Ender's Game* by Orson Scott Card
- *Fahrenheit 451* by Ray Bradbury
- "Harrison Bergeron" by Kurt Vonnegut
- "The Lottery" by Shirley Jackson
- *The Time Machine* by H. G. Wells
- *V for Vendetta* by Alan Moore and David Lloyd

A group of books with a similar theme can also throw light on Big Ideas. Big Ideas worth considering include the following:

- What makes a community?
- What does the community owe the individual and vice versa?
- How can individuals best respond when a community is or becomes unjust or otherwise damaging to individuals' interests?

Answer Pages

Possible responses are given in the **Answer Pages**. The responses include critical analysis of the novel that you may find useful. Students' answers are expected to be more developed than the sample answers in many cases.

TEACHING WITH DIGITAL EDITIONS

One of the advantages of many digital editions is the ready access to definitions of every word, but there are three reasons that it is not wise to rely on this in place of teaching vocabulary: 1) it interrupts the reader's experience of the story; 2) the definition offered may not match the use in the text; 3) the word may not appear (for example, Collins's neologisms). On the other hand, digital editions may allow adjustment of brightness, font, text size, and line length, giving the reader more control over the reading experience, and may also allow note-taking. The device may be able to read the book aloud, but you may wish to check the quality of this feature.

INTRODUCING THE LITERATURE

How you choose to introduce the literature will likely depend on the student and reading mode. For Aesthetic/Analytic reading, you may simply hand the student an edition and allow the author to unfold the world of the story in his or her own way. To prepare students to read the work aesthetically, explain that in a work of fiction, an author creates an imaginary world. An important task in beginning a literature selection is coming to terms with that world.

Notes to the Teacher

Notes to the Teacher

When students need guidance and when you are teaching analysis, you can use this guide to help students contextualize *Catching Fire* using Strategy 1: Beginning the Second Book in a Series, p. 11). If you are reading the entire trilogy, you may already know what familiarity students have with the series and author and, if it seems appropriate, correct any misapprehensions students have, e.g., conclusions drawn from the movies don't fit the books. You may wish to specifically encourage students to—as much as they can—set aside what they know from outside sources and read the text on its own terms.

Whatever mode students are using, it is a good idea to point out that it is possible to consciously assess one's own understanding and that this process is called *metacognitive reflection*. Also point out that doing so may interrupt the experience of the story until such reflection becomes seamlessly integrated into the reader's process. You may wish to review the process by modeling with a think-aloud approach as you go through questions 3–5 in Strategy 1 (for aesthetic reading, skip over the others for now). Simply read aloud the portion of *Catching Fire* (or another book, if you don't want to influence students' reading) needed to answer the questions, and speak aloud your thoughts as you formulate your responses, making explicit the connections and prior knowledge you are developing in your thoughts. Continue with whichever prereading activities you have determined are appropriate.

Sample Lesson Plan

It's likely that students will eventually end up reading chapter-by-chapter. If they are using the aesthetic/analytic approach, this will be their second reading of the book. At this point, all students can engage in prereading, during reading, and after reading activities geared for their abilities and needs.

Prereading Activities: Choose these activities based on how much prereading guidance students need and what can be handled after they read. Prereading activities may include:

- previewing vocabulary and doing a vocabulary exercise;
- reviewing the developments of the previous chapter(s); and
- reviewing predictions.

During Reading: Students can read with their Reading Journals handy, if it suits their reading mode: if they are experiencing the story and don't want to be interrupted to do a journal entry, allow them to write in the journal after they read. If students need guidance as they read, you may wish to give them some of the journal and discussion topics before they read to help focus their attention. Additional journal activities they can use with every chapter include the following:

- recording questions they have about what they have read;
- recording associations they have made between this text and other texts, experiences, or situations; and
- taking notes on the images and/or feelings the text evoked.

After Reading: Students can complete the Journal and Discussion Topics, and the Writer's Forum and Strategy Pages and Test (if any). You may wish to end each discussion by having students explain and note their predictions

Adding a Social Dimension

If you'd like to add a social dimension to your literature classes, I recommend the Subtext app for iPad, which will allow you to purchase *Catching Fire* from Google Books from within the app and have a private reading experience with your class, while providing a forum for tracking literary elements, making predictions, noting emotions, taking polls, etc. Since students will have access to others' comments, you may want to have them read chapters on their own first, to avoid interrupting their initial reading experience. For more information, go to http://subtext.com.

SUZANNE COLLINS AND THE HUNGER GAMES TRILOGY

Collins was born in Connecticut in 1962, but the fact that her father was in the military meant that her childhood was spent at a number of locations in the U.S. and overseas. A military historian, her father shared his understandings of the world with his children, so Collins grew up with an awareness of war. After spending a number of years writing for children's television shows, she met James Proimos, an author of children's books, who inspired her and to whom *The Hunger Games* is dedicated. Her fantasy series *The Underland Chronicles* was published between 2003 and 2007 and treats war in a variety of ways. *The Hunger Games* trilogy, the first novel of which was published in 2008, progresses from a war game in the first book, to a revolution in the second, and a war in the third.

The story of *The Hunger Games* sprang from several roots. On the one hand, Collins—a fan of Greek mythology—was influenced by the story of King Minos of Crete imposing a yearly tribute of seven youths and seven maidens on Athens, and thrusting them into the Labyrinth, where they were slain by the Minotaur. Theseus, son of the king of Athens goes as one of the seven youths, slays the Minotaur, and ends the practice. On the other hand, an incident of channel surfing during which she was going back and forth between a reality TV program and real war coverage and the two began to blend in her mind was another source of inspiration. Collins identified Spartacus as an inspiration for the overall shape of the series.

THE HUNGER GAMES MOVIES

Collins contributed to the screenplays for the movie versions of *The Hunger Games* (2012) and *Catching Fire* (2013), and the differences between the books and the movies are likely to come up as you teach the novel. Collins herself pointed to three important differences in an interview with Scholastic, and although she was talking about the first movie, these concerns certainly influence the second:

> **Q: We understand you worked on the initial screenplay for a film to be based on *The Hunger Games* What is the biggest difference between writing a novel and writing a screenplay?**
>
> A: There were several significant differences. Time, for starters. When you're adapting a novel into a two-hour movie you can't take everything with you. The story has to be condensed to fit the new form. Then there's the question of how best to take a book told in the first person and present tense and transform it into a satisfying dramatic experience. In the novel, you never leave Katniss for a second and are privy to all of her thoughts so you need a way to dramatize her inner world and to make it possible for other characters to exist outside of her company. Finally, there's the challenge of how to present the violence while still maintaining a PG-13 rating so that your core audience can view it. A lot of things are acceptable on a page that wouldn't be on a screen. But how certain moments are depicted will ultimately be in the director's hands.
>
> (http://www.scholastic.com/thehungergames/media/suzanne_collins_q_and_q.pdf)

So, students who have seen the movies and try to avoid reading the book are likely to make mistakes in point of view, leaving out details, and providing different descriptions of the violence. As of this writing, the movie version of *Catching Fire* has not been released, but the very first image in the trailer (which I suggest you avoid watching if you have not seen the movie) shows a perspective that Katniss cannot see, suggesting that—like the movie of *The Hunger Games*—the movie of *Catching Fire* does not maintain the first-person point of view of Katniss. Later, the trailer shows more material that Katniss is not party to (discussions between Plutarch Heavensbee) and has changes to the confrontation between Katniss and Thread after Gale is whipped. One way to dispel the movie's influence is to help students analyze the movie so thoroughly that they gain a detailed understanding of how (and why) it differs from the book: this makes it much easier to keep the two separate.

Notes to the Teacher

Common Core

The Common Core State Standards Initiative proposes educational standards that aim to "provide a consistent, clear understanding of what students are expected to learn, so teachers and parents know what they need to do to help them." As of October 2013, 45 states and four US territories have adopted the Common Core State Standards. The following chart shows how exercises and activities in this teaching guide align with the relevant Common Core State Standards. Because this guide may be used across a range of ages and grade levels, the chart refers to the key content of each standard across grades 6–12.

The Common Core State Standards emphasize skills and knowledge, so you may wonder why this teaching guide emphasizes *strategies* and how strategies and skills are related. A *strategy* is the knowledge of when and how to deploy your skills for the most effective results. If you have skills and don't know when and how to use them, they don't do much good. The strategy lessons in this teaching guide provide instruction in skills, contextualized with information about when and how to use them effectively.

STANDARD	PAGE NUMBER
Reading Standards for Literature	
1. Cite textual evidence	12, 17, 40, 43, 46, 47, 50, 53, 54, 55, 71, 73, 74, 76, 79, 81, 86, 87
2. Determine themes	85, 86, 88–9
3. Analyze story development	character development 16; plot development 19; character motivation and choices, 20, 40; contribution of setting, 22; characterization, 29; Chekhov's Gun trope, 63
4. Determine meanings of words	tone (including irony), 12, 38, 60, 84; impact of description, 31; figurative language, 34, 36, 52, 60; symbols, motifs, and allusions, 36; meaning of words, 46, 47, 64, 66, 67, 73, 87; diction, 57
5. Analyze structure	book and series levels, 11, 14–15, 16, 33; recap, 14, 19, 45; flashbacks, 16, 19; foreshadowing, 19, 71; setting, 22; parallels and repetition, 30, 45, 47, 50, 55, 60, 63, 64, 70, 71, 85, 86, 88–9; cliffhangers and shockers, 49
6. Analyze point of view/narration	13, 15, 24, 27, 31, 33, 35, 38, 47, 50, 52, 53, 54, 57, 60, 64, 73, 81, 83, 84
7. Compare multiple versions	41, 86
9. Compare/contrast texts	Text compared with: *The Hunger Games*, 12, 13, 17, 30, 45, 60, 66, 84, 86 "Wild Swans at Coole," 24; The Bill of Rights, 25–6, 41; "Terrorism and the Uses of Terror," 26; "To the Virgins, to Make Much of Time," 67; brief quotations, 88–89
Writing Standards	
1. Write arguments to support claims	12, 17, 40, 43, 47, 50, 55, 67, 71, 74, 79, 81, 87
2. Write informative/explanatory texts	12, 17, 24, 27, 31, 35, 37, 38, 41, 42, 43, 46, 47, 50, 52, 55, 57, 60, 61, 64, 66, 67, 68, 69, 70, 71, 73, 74, 76, 78, 79, 81, 87
3. Write narratives	67, 71
9. Draw evidence from literary texts	12, 13, 17, 24, 30, 45, 60, 66, 67, 84, 86, and passim
10. Write a range of texts for various purposes/audiences	translating narrative into drama, 23; comparing/contrasting books in a series, 30; short research report, 37; investigation, 42; letter of farewell, 59; eulogy/anecdote, 67; possible ending, 71; instructions/directions, 78; comparison of two treatments of the same story, 86
Language Standards	
5. Understand figurative language, word relationships, and nuances	11, 34, 36, 52, 60, 63, 87,

Strategy 1

Plot—Beginning the Second Book in a Trilogy

Beginning the second book in a series has its own particular demands. On the one hand, you have prior knowledge from the first book (and maybe other books by the same author, as well). You know the genre and a good deal about the world of the book, the characters, the themes, the narrator, and more. You may have explicit knowledge about some of the plot developments that are coming up, or at least some pretty shrewd guesses.

But two types of problems can arise right off the bat when you start the second book in a series. It may have been awhile since you read the first book, so elements of the first book that the author refers to in the second book may slip by you. Or you may have seen a movie or game version that has melded with your memory of the book, so that you're not quite sure which is which in some cases. These issues are fairly simple to address: all you have to do is reread the first book right before you pick up the second. If you've only read the first book once, you may actually discover some points that you missed the first time around and/or identify some patterns or themes that weren't clear to you previously.

There's another aspect of beginning a second book and that is its place in the whole. A second book in a series of seven—for example, *Harry Potter and the Chamber of Secrets*—plays a different role in the overall plot than the second book in a trilogy, like *Catching Fire*. But our knowledge of the role of this book goes even further because we know—from Collins's background as a television writer, her discussion of plot in interviews, and simply by looking at the division of the series and each book—that Collins structured her work with reference to a three-act structure. This means that each book has two levels of plot: it works as a three-act structure in itself, and it works as an act of the larger three-act structure of the trilogy, making *Catching Fire* function as Act Two. (See Strategy 2: Understanding the Series Reading Process, p. 14 for more on this topic.)

1. Review the first book of the trilogy, *The Hunger Games*, as Act One of the whole by identifying the genre, narrator, protagonist(s), antagonist(s), the inciting incident, and the reversal.

2. Based on the information from *The Hunger Games* that you identified in question 1, describe your expectations for *Catching Fire*.

3. Think about the title *Catching Fire*. Based on the title and your prior knowledge from *The Hunger Games*, what do you expect to happen in this book?

4. What can you tell about the story from the part titles: Part I: "The Spark"; Part II: "The Quell"; Part III: "The Enemy"? How do they seem to relate to the book title? How do they seem to relate to the titles of the three parts of *The Hunger Games*: Part I: "The Tributes"; Part II: "The Games"; Part III "The Victor"?

5. Read the first three paragraphs. Identify each reference, attitude, etc. that you understand more deeply because you've already read *The Hunger Games*.

6. Given everything you know at this point, what do you predict will happen in Act Two of this trilogy? What do you think the confrontation will involve? What do you predict will be the reversal?

Directions:
First, read the information. Then, answer the question or questions.

Catching Fire: A Teaching Guide 11

Chapter 1

PART I "THE SPARK"
Back in District 12

Vocabulary

scaling 3 climbing
cater to 3 provide for
beautify 3 make more lovely
loathe 4 feel strong hatred for
clocked in 4 punched the time clock at the start of a work shift
contracted 5 become ill with
saplings 6 young trees
triggers 6 levers to activate a mechanism
inescapable 6 fashioned to prevent escape
instinct 6 inborn sense; natural understanding
designated 6 assigned
squat 6 literal: short and broad; slang: small and worthless
stowed 7 hid away for future use
hearth 7 floor of a fireplace; symbolic of home and family life
mourn 7 recall w/ sadness and longing
interwoven 7 w/ all parts linked closely together
retrospect 7 looking back
scruffy 7 not well-groomed; untidy; dirty
entitled 8 gave the legal right
provocation 8 encouragement
salve 8 healing ointment
bulk 9 greater part, majority
black market 9 illegal market that avoids legal restrictions
withdrawal 10 symptoms caused by ceasing to take an addictive substance
stockpiling 10 getting and saving extra
gourd 11 edible fruit w/ a hard skin, related to pumpkin and squash
law enforcers 11 members of government department who enforce the laws
affixed 13 attached
groundskeeper 13 person who cares for and maintains lawns and gardens
exudes 13 gives off; projects
brace myself 13 prepare for unpleasantness or danger
droppings 13 animal excrement
intermingled 13 mixed together
stench 13 strong, foul smell
sprawled 13 spread out awkwardly
unearth 13 dig out from deep in a pile
coax 14 tend something in order to make it behave as desired
guttural 14 harsh and from deep in the throat
pried 14 removed by force
profanity 14 language that is offensive because it is abusive, vulgar, takes God's name in vain, or a combination of those
douses 15 pours (a large amount of) liquid over
homecoming 15 a notable return home after trials or a long journey
tailored 16 well-cut and/or made-to-order (as opposed to "off the rack" or mass-produced)
lovebirds 17 couple who demonstrate their affection publicly
ushered 17 guided; escorted
reassuring 17 meant to restore confidence
itinerary 17 planned route and stops on a journey
vaguely 17 in an unclear or indistinct way

Journal and Discussion Topics

1. Now that you've read the first chapter, what do you think Part I of this story will be about? What evidence supports your conclusions?
2. Katniss estimates that the odds for evading a wild dog attack are not in her favor (p. 3). What does the way she phrases her concern about the dogs suggest about her worldview? Compare this to her use of the same phrase (with Gale) in Chapter 1 of *The Hunger Games* (*HG* pp. 7–8): what has changed?
3. How would Katniss like to treat the Hunger Games? What prevents her from doing this?
4. How and why has the role of hunting in Katniss's life changed?
5. What are Gale's talents? How do you think they could feature in the rest of the story?
6. How does Collins convey Katniss's discomfort with her new life?
7. Compare and contrast Katniss's shopping in *The Hunger Games* and in Chapter 1 of *Catching Fire*.
8. How would you characterize Katniss's relationships with the Peacekeepers she meets in Chapter 1?
9. Since Katniss lives next-door to a baker, why would she buy buns at the Hob?
10. Why does Greasy Sae refer to Gale as Katniss's cousin?
11. What does the description of Haymitch and his house convey to you about him?

12 *Catching Fire: A Teaching Guide*

12. Describe the state of Katniss's relationship to Peeta.
13. Go to the Miss America website http://www.missamerica.org/competition-info/faq.aspx and read the first three questions and answers to gain an idea about what Miss America does during the year after she is selected. Compare and contrast this with the tour of the victor(s) of the Hunger Games.
14. What signals alert Katniss to the fact that something is wrong when she returns home?
15. Why does President Snow smell of blood and roses, do you think?
16. Summarize the chapter from Mrs. Everdeen's point of view. Be sure to tell only what she knows or could reasonably be expected to know.

Summary

Sixteen-year-old Katniss Everdeen, the first-person narrator, is spending the pre-dawn hours in the woods, dreading the beginning of the Victory Tour, for which her preparation will begin by noon. It is six months after the Hunger Games from which Katniss emerged as one of the Victors, and the Capitol forces Victors to visit all the Districts to keep the horror of the Games alive throughout the year. She is alone because Gale now works in the mines. Katniss reflects on her fear of the mines, worsened by the death of her father in them, and on her changed relationship with Gale, since he has to work and since she won the Games.

Having gotten a good haul from the traps, Katniss heads back to District 12, crossing the non-functioning electrified fence, and heading to her old house to change before dropping off Gale's share of the game to his mother, Hazelle. A comment Hazelle makes about Gale's liking to save his Sundays to see Katniss both makes her blush and recalls to her mind the fact that the romance with fellow tribute Peeta Mellark—real on his side; carried out with mixed motivations on hers—has changed things between Katniss and Gale. That the romance with Peeta must reemerge for the tour makes Katniss feel anxious.

Next, Katniss stops by the Hob, the local black market, where she spends some of her Victor's reward in an effort to spread the wealth around and purchases white liquor for Haymitch. When Cray, the Head Peacekeeper, expresses disapproval, she tells him it's for medicinal purposes. She purchases some soup from Greasy Sae, and is teased good-naturedly by Darius, a young Peacekeeper. Greasy Sae's question about whether Gale will get to see her off leads Katniss to explain how the conceit of Gale being Katniss's cousin came about.

As it starts to snow, Katniss heads back to the Victor's Village where she and her family now live, stopping in at Haymitch's house to wake him. After a few failed efforts, she dumps ice water on his head, leaping out of the way as he springs to his feet with a knife in his hand. Peeta arrives, bringing bread, and the interchange between the two is awkward. Heading home, Katniss is met at the door by her mother who tells her she has a visitor. A man from the Capitol escorts her to the door of the study, and upon opening it, she discovers President Snow, smelling of blood and roses.

Chapter 1, cont

Catching Fire: A Teaching Guide 13

Strategy 2

Understanding the Series Reading Process

So what's different about reading a series than reading a stand-alone book? It partly depends on the type of series it is. Some series are episodic, each book telling of a particular episode in a more-or-less static character's life. In this type of series, the following are generally true:

- There is no character development and characters don't age.
- Each book has a self-contained plot.
- Any references to other series books can be overlooked.
- Because of these three factors, order isn't important, for the most part.

The original Nancy Drew and Tom Swift series are both good examples, as are many long-running comic book stories, like those featuring Archie Andrews or superheroes, such as Superman.

But other series have character arcs—a planned course of character development— and a story that develops across titles, like the Hunger Games trilogy. These series make sense in only one, set order.

When reading a series with character development and a continuing plot, there are several factors that differ from reading a standalone book:

- character arcs with greater complexity
- dependence on material in earlier books
- two levels of plot: book and series

Character Arcs

In a series, there is more room for a complex character arc—one that doesn't always move in a smooth upward direction. In a series in which characters experiences trauma, as in Collins' trilogy, those characters may suffer regressions—becoming less mature and capable of dealing with the world and returning to an earlier stage of development—as well as make progress. This can make the character arc more complex, so keep an eye out for retreats as well as advances in character development in a series that is not simply episodic.

Earlier Material

There are various ways that a subsequent book in a series can make use of earlier material. Recapping earlier events is typical in subsequent books, and Collins uses this technique (see Strategy 4: Plot—Identifying Flashback, Recap, and Foreshadowing, p. 19). There may also be unflagged references to material from earlier books that the author depends on the reader noticing and identifying. For example, when Katniss mentions Buttercup (p. 7), the reader is expected to recall, without being told, Katniss's initial exposition about Buttercup (*HG* pp. 3–4) and be able to draw conclusions about the change in their relationship.

Another way that material from previous books in a series is used is to fulfill or subvert (undermine) reader expectations that were developed in the previous book. If the reader doesn't remember and have conscious expectations, that reader won't have the experience the author intended.

Directions:
First, read the information. Then, answer the question or questions.

Two Levels of Plot

When a book is part of a series, the author plots it on two levels—the book level and the series level—adding a layer of complexity to plot analysis. When reading the first book of a series, it is difficult to analyze on the series level, because there isn't enough information. It is only when one has read the entire series that one can clearly see the role the first book played.

Another important result of books being constructed as parts of a series is that, until the final volume, the endings are not true endings: they finish off one section of the story but do not have the finality of the ending of a stand-alone book or the ending of the final book in a series.

The key techniques for addressing these elements of the series reading process are:

- reading the series all at once, in order or rereading the previous book(s) prior to reading the next book;
- keeping earlier books handy for reference;
- paying attention to material that fits with or dispels your earlier hypotheses.

A digital edition of an earlier book can be particularly useful for locating information from earlier in the series, especially in books, such as Collins's, that have no chapter titles. Simply choose a key word and search.

Strategy 2, cont.

1. In *third-person limited point of view*, the main character—the one from whose perspective the story is told by the narrator—is often named and described to some degree in a paragraph or several close to the beginning of the book. In a series, this information is already known, but it is often repeated in every book in case readers have forgotten since reading the previous volume.

   But this approach would be awkward in a series with *first-person narration*. Explain how the first-person narrator reiterates basic facts about herself in Chapter 1 of *Catching Fire*.

   - her name
   - her (changing) location
   - her family members
   - her appearance

2. How does a knowledge of the interactions between Katniss and Buttercup in *The Hunger Games* (pp. 3–4) inform your understanding of Katniss's interactions with Buttercup in *Catching Fire* (p. 7)?

3. If a reader didn't recall the sentence about the odds being in one's favor from *The Hunger Games*, how would his or her understanding of the first paragraph of *Catching Fire* be diminished?

4. Reread the last two paragraphs of *The Hunger Games*. Consider what expectations it raises for the beginning of *Catching Fire*. Were these expectations fulfilled or subverted? Explain your answer. Then tell how a reader's experience would be different without this expectation.

5. What expectations does Chapter 1 create for you about the plot of *Catching Fire*?

Strategy 3
Charting Character Development

English anthropologist and linguist Gregory Bateson pointed out in the introduction to his book *Mind and Nature* that things cannot be defined in themselves alone: Understanding their relationship(s) to their context(s) is an essential part of knowing what they are. In the specific case of understanding character, it is often, if not always, true that the development of character can be marked by the character's changing role in the community. It is certainly true in this trilogy. We're going to use this insight to gauge character development. But to do so, we need to understand the event of Katniss's life in chronological order.

Collins often uses flashbacks for exposition, as we saw in *HG* Strategy 7: Plot—Foreshadowing and Flashback. This means that events do not unfold in time order, but in a sequence designed to meet other narrative concerns. To understand Katniss's development in terms of her community, it is essential to review the events of the series in time order. So we need to recast them using appropriate time periods. You can employ the following technique to explore character development in any complex book.

1. Use the plot details from *The Hunger Games* through the first chapter of *Catching Fire* to create a timeline of key events, adding to it as you continue to read. Use time periods that correspond to Katniss's age, such as:

   - younger than (<) age 11,
   - age 11,
   - ages 12–15,
   - age 16 in *The Hunger Games* (*HG),* and
   - age 16 in *Catching Fire* (*CF)*

   For example,
   - <11: Mr. Everdeen taught Katniss to hunt.
   - 11: Mr. Everdeen died in a mine explosion.

2. Use your timeline to help you analyze the development of Katniss's key relationships, which should help shed light on her personal development. The relationships you should examine are those with Prim, Gale, Peeta, Haymitch, District 12 residents, and Other Districts. Here is a sample analysis of Katniss's development in relation to her mother up to the end of Chapter 1 of *Catching Fire*:

Mother: After an apparently normal relationship until age 11, Katniss responds to Mrs. Everdeen's deep depression following Mr. Everdeen's death by taking on the parental role until her mother recovers. As her mother returns to work as a healer, she becomes stronger, and regains Prim's trust, though not Katniss's. As *CF* begins, Mrs. Everdeen seems to have capably prepared the house for the Victory Tour and manages to signal to Katniss to prevent her mentioning where she's been when she returns from hunting at the end of Chapter 1.

Follow this model and extend your analysis as you continue to read, keeping in mind that character arcs can include regression—a return to a previous, less developed state.

3. Review your analyses of Katniss's relationships as a group. What conclusions can you draw? Look for patterns, trends, and signs of development or backtracking.

Directions:
First, read the information. Then, answer the question or questions.

Chapter 2   A Visit from the President

Vocabulary

jarring 18 startling; shocking
consequently 18 as a result
undermined 18 weakened or destroyed indirectly
decrees 18 makes an official pronouncement
audacity 18 boldness with a disregard for convention and consequences
mutual understanding 19 knowledge that people share and know that they share
intruder 19 person who is present w/out permission
ambiguous 20 open to multiple interpretations
sentimental 20 tendency to be swayed by emotions, especially romantic feelings
streak 20 personal trait; element of character
lapel 20 An extension of a jacket collar that folds back along the front neckline
play out . . . scenario 21 act through the logical consequences of the setup
uprising 21 a popular revolt against a government, used here to refer to a minor action that is short of a full-scale revolution
prophetic 23 able to accurately predict the future
revulsion 24 violent disgust; strong negative reaction that makes one recoil
resolution 24 conclusion; agreed upon course of action
implication 24 suggestion that is not directly stated; inference
obligatory 25 required by law
Parcel 25 goods wrapped in a package
tins 25 cans
intricate 27 complex; very complicated and requiring dedicated effort
endangered 28 caused danger to
dynamic 28 style of interaction
thereby 28 and as a result; and by that means
averted 29 prevented
flinch 29 startle or wince due to surprise, pain, or fear and w/out conscious thought

Journal and Discussion Topics

1. Katniss compares President Snow to a viper. In *The Hunger Games* on p. 175, she also refers to vipers. How are the two "viper situations" parallel?
2. Katniss says different things in different places about her motivation in taking the action she did with the berries. What does Katniss say about her motivation in Chapter 2 (pp. 18–20). Do you find her statements to be consistent? Explain.
3. Why do you think President Snow makes the suggestion to Katniss that they not lie to each other?
4. What do you think would have happened if Seneca Crane had decided to blow Katniss and Peeta "to dust" when she pulled out the berries? Why do you think President Snow chooses to say what he does about Crane's choice and the consequences of letting the scenario play out?
5. A *monopsony* (from the Greek *monos* - "single" and *opsonein* - "purchase provisions") is a market in which a single buyer controls the market and prices. It is essentially a buyer's monopoly. If you consider the Capitol as having a monopsony and combine that with what you know about the division of industry in Panem, what light does it shed on the relationship between the Capitol and the districts and on President Snow's remarks about the country's fragility?
6. Katniss says she's struck by the "sincerity" of President Snow's comments. Do you think this is an accurate assessment? Provide evidence to support your view.
7. If you were President Snow, would you tell Katniss what she means to others in Panem? What do you imagine is his reason for doing so?
8 How do you think President Snow gets information that you or Katniss didn't expect him to have?
9. What is the effect of Katniss making comments about both Gale's and President Snow's lips in the same chapter?
10. What do you think of President Snow's plan of action for Katniss? Explain why you think as you do.
11. Summarize the chapter by identifying all the ways in which President Snow exerts power over Katniss in this chapter.

Chapter 2
Page 18

Catching Fire: A Teaching Guide   17

Chapter 2, cont.

Summary

Given both her history with President Snow and what she knows of standard Tour protocol, Katniss concludes that his visit means that she's in trouble. She reviews in her mind the reasons he has to be displeased with her, as she stands stock still, waiting for him to speak. He starts by suggesting that they not lie to each other, and Katniss agrees. He then muses about how he expects Katniss to behave, implying that any lack of cooperation will be taken out on her family and "cousins," and then invites Katniss to sit. He tells Katniss, with apparent sincerity, how her use of the poisonous berries—compounded by Head Gamemaker Seneca Crane's choice not to destroy both Katniss and Peeta rather than declare them both victors—and her "love-crazed schoolgirl" act convinced Capitol residents, but not everyone in the districts, who have taken her use of the berries as an act of defiance and a model. There have not yet been uprisings, he says, but they will come about, and even lead to revolution if things do not change. Revolution would have dire consequences for the districts because "the entire system" would collapse as a result. Katniss—who has pinned down the source of the roses smell to the flower in his lapel but doesn't know where the smell of blood comes from—comments on the fragility of a regime that a handful of berries can undermine, but Snow counters that its fragility is not what Katniss supposes.

Katniss's mother brings in tea and cookies that Peeta has decorated. When she leaves, Katniss states that she didn't mean to start any uprisings. Snow says he believes her, but it's irrelevant because Cinna's costume design was prophetic: an unattended spark may grow to an "inferno that destroys Panem." Katniss asks him to tell her what he wants her to do, and he says it's not that simple.

A remark about the cookies brings Peeta into the conversation. Snow says he is not the only person who has doubts about her love for Peeta. He then threatens to kill Gale, leading Katniss to reminisce about the events when she returned home. Her memories include the first of 12 Parcel Days on which food is delivered to everyone in the district, the one time Gale kissed her during their first private meeting in the woods after her return, and the fact that she's been cool to Peeta and made her preference for Gale obvious. She begs Snow not to hurt Gale and says he's just her friend. Snow claims to only be interested in Gale to the extent that his existence impacts Katniss's interactions with Peeta, and thus, the mood of the districts. Katniss promises she will act in a way to convince the districts, and Snow—saying that she must convince him as well—tells her that the Tour is her one shot to reverse the growing issues. As he walks to the study door, he whispers in Katniss's ear that he knows about the kiss.

18   Catching Fire: A Teaching Guide

Strategy 4

Plot—Analyzing the Use of Flashback, Recap, and Foreshadowing

Writers have a variety of motivations for shifting the timeline, either to recount earlier material or to provide hints or speculation about what will happen later. **Flashback** and **recap** are two ways of introducing material from earlier in the story line. **Foreshadowing** is a way of giving the reader clues about what is going to happen later in the story. Such clues may reward the observant reader when they prove true, or surprise the reader if they are misleading. We introduced them in the *HG* teaching guide, but now we're going to focus on the writer's purposes for using them.

Writers use **flashbacks** to take material out of time sequence, inserting an account of events that occurred prior to the current moment in the story. Flashbacks are often part of the exposition of the novel, providing essential background information that is out of time-order sequence. A flashback may be fit into the narrative because a character's memory is jogged, because of a direct comment or question, or by the need to tell another character about an earlier occurrence. Flashback material is new to the reader, so may shed new light on the hows and whys of what the reader already knows, filling in what the reader may or may not have recognized as incomplete information.

Recap differs from flashback in being the repetition of earlier material that the reader has already read. You will almost always find recapping in the first chapter of any book in a series other than the first. Recapping can also occur through the narrator's or another character's recollection of an earlier incident. This could happen for a variety of reasons. For example, when there is any mystery involved in the story (even if the story does not fit the mystery, detective, or crime genres), writers use recap to reiterate clues or red herrings that they want to bring more strongly to the reader's attention. Highly charged events, or those with important effects may be recapped as a foundation for a further exploration of their impact.

Collins, unlike many other writers, often integrates new information into her recaps. For example, it is only in Katniss's recap of her trip to the Hob in Chapter 1 that we learn that in between being a warehouse and a black market, it was a place where people met to conduct illegal trades. This fact is never mentioned in *The Hunger Games*.

Foreshadowing is narration that touches on things that have not yet happened, a prediction of what will take place. It is often used to create anticipation for the reader—and then fulfill expectations or subvert (undermine) them. In a story with an unreliable narrator, such as Katniss, foreshadowing should be considered with caution.

When you come upon out-of-order material, examine its purpose to determine if its informative or unreliable, meant to lead you astray.

1. Although Collins recaps some information about Gale from *The Hunger Games* in Chapter 1, she also presents some new information. Identify the information that is new. Explain why she might have chosen to mix recap and new material.

2. Review the first two chapters of *Catching Fire* to find one instance of **foreshadowing**, two instances of **flashback**, and three instances of **recap** (besides the instance mentioned in question 1). Identify the page numbers and beginning words of each sentence or passage you identify. What purpose do they serve?

Directions: First, read the information. Then, answer the question or questions.

Catching Fire: A Teaching Guide 19

Strategy 5 — Analyzing Choices

Here is a 4-part Choice Analysis Tool to use in understanding choices in *Catching Fire*. Part 1 is for analyzing the situation, Part 2 for analyzing motivation (why people make the choices they do), Part 3 for analyzing the decision maker's access to reliable information, and Part 4 for analyzing the finality of the choice.

1. Select one or more appropriate items from each part of the Choice Analysis Tool to characterize how President Snow coerces Katniss's choices in Chapter 2 of *Catching Fire*.

PART 1—TYPES OF CHOICES

Free Choice (Voluntary)
A decision with no limitations or constraints from anyone or anything
- A *pet owner* decides to name her gerbil *Wally*, rather than *Rudolfus*.

Offer (Voluntary)
A decision in which some alternative possibility with no strings or pressure is considered and freely chosen
- A *commuter* accepts a ride from a neighbor headed in the same direction rather than walk.

Constrained Choice (Voluntary within the constrained circumstances)
A decision in which there is some limitation caused by resources or the situation (such as money, time, other peoples' taste), but no threat
- A *teen* watches a movie online instead of going to the theatre. ($/time/transportation)

Bargain (Voluntary)
A decision in which two or more people come to a mutual agreement without threat, and with or without compromise
- A *man* agrees to lunch with a colleague who has a 2-for-1 deal at an expensive restaurant on the understanding that they will split the bill.

Choice w/ Spelled-Out Consequences (Voluntary)
A decision in which choices are curtailed by the consequences, which may be arbitrary, but do not violate the decision-maker's rights and are presented as fact, not threat
- A *woman* having a garage sale wants to sell a CD for $8. A shopper says she won't spend more than $6 for it.

Exploitive Choice (Either Voluntary-Under-the-Circumstances or Involuntary)
A choice is offered that takes advantage of a power differential and the fact that the chooser is not in a position to bargain.
- A *person* with no unemployment benefits and no other job prospects is offered a job for wages that are less that the value of his labor.

Coerced Choice (Either Voluntary-Under-the-Circumstances or Involuntary)
A decision that is influenced by a credible threat, with the consequence for non-compliance being unwelcome and violating the coerced person's rights/freedom.
- A *person* is told by a blackmailer to pay a certain sum or the illegal thing the person did will be shared with the police.

Terrorized Choice (Either Voluntary-Under-the-Circumstances or Involuntary)
A decision that is not only influenced by a credible threat that violates the person's rights and is unwelcome, but is made more credible by the fact that harm has or is currently being caused or physical force is being used, so that the person's rights/freedom are already violated in unwelcome ways.s
- A *person* being held hostage is commanded to rob a bank or lose his/her life.

Directions: First, read the information. Then, answer the question or questions.

PART 2—MOTIVATIONS/INTENTIONS/DESIRES

Seeking a good for oneself
> *Life*
>> Food and Water
>> Shelter
>> Safety
>> Sleep
>> Health/Healthcare
>> Equality
>
> *Liberty*
>> Freedom from coercion and terrorism
>> Rational, predictable, fair, honest treatment by the state
>> Justice
>> Self-Direction
>
> *Happiness*
>> Become Educated
>> Achieve Accomplishments
>>> (e.g., Attain Physical Prowess, Succeed in a Career, Attain and Exercise Authority)
>>
>> Acquire and Own Property
>> Gain Status Corresponding to Accomplishments
>> Enjoy Love/Friendship/Family
>> Express one's Feelings
>> Create Beauty
>> Reach a Satisfied Emotional State
>>> (e.g., Take a Vacation, Go for a Walk in Nature)
>>
>> Enjoy Entertainment
>> Build Community

Seeking a good for specific other person
> Same as good for self, more or less

Seeking a good for the community
> Same as good for self, more or less

Seeking a Theoretical Good
> Doing the right thing by practicing a virtue or following a rule, law, or belief
> Keeping a promise or fulfilling another type of obligation or responsibility

(Any of the above can be carried out to excess/immoderately, illegally, or with disregard for others or to the detriment of others; some can be carried out inadequately.)

PART 3—INFORMATION LEVEL AND AWARENESS

Level of Information

No Information
Partial Information
Complete Information

Awareness of Level of Information

Aware
Partially Aware
Unaware
Mistaken in awareness of level

Quality of Information

True
False
  Misinformation
  Lies
  Invalid Conclusions
  Wishful Thinking

PART 4—EXTENT OF CHOICE

Final Choice
Non-Final Choice
  Choice Made in Stages
  Retracted Choice
  Revised Choice

Strategy 5, cont.

Strategy 6

Analyzing Control of the Setting

Setting refers to both the world in which the story takes place and the changing scenery that serves as the backdrop for each individual scene or chapter. Setting includes what the characters can sense in their environment, for example,

- time of day
- season of the year
- plants and animals
- natural features
- weather
- landscape
- buildings or other structures
- human-made features

Settings may be a mere backdrop to the story, or it may have a more integral part, and it can serve different functions even within one story. The setting may be symbolic or reveal information about characters. Katniss's and Buttercup's preference for their old home in the Seam as opposed to their new home in the Victor's Village (pp. 6–7) provides some insight into Katniss's character and increases the parallels between her and Buttercup.

Setting may also create conflicts for the characters; help or hinder the characters in achieving their goal(s); provide materials or resources that help the characters solve problems; or create physical hardships or challenges that are difficult to overcome. We have already seen that in the arena, setting can be both a means of survival and something approaching a weapon of mass destruction (for example, the Gamemaker-made flames, *HG* pp. 172–174).

The settings of a story and how the settings function affect how we and the characters feel about their surroundings. This feeling is called **mood**, and you can use your mood to gain insight into the purpose of the setting. For example, a setting that makes you anxious creates suspense.

More than in many other books, the settings are an important factor in the Hunger Games trilogy, and control of the setting is key. For example, the Gamemakers put a river into the arena. Peeta took control of his setting by blending in with it, camouflaging himself to look like part of the riverbank, which saved his life. The Gamemakers put poisonous berries in the arena to kill tributes. Katniss took control of the setting by using the berries in a way the Gamemakers didn't anticipate to save herself and Peeta. So, for our reading of *Catching Fire*, we're going to focus on control of the setting, both inside and outside the arena.

1. For Chapters 1–2, record instances of control over the setting (both the characters' location and what they do in their locations) and who exercises that control. Add other chapters after you've read them.

Chapter	Instance of Control	Who Controls?
1	Katniss activities in woods	Katniss
1	Katniss visiting Hazelle, the Hob	Katniss

Directions:
First, read the information. Then, answer the question or questions.

Writer's Forum 1

Translating Fiction Into Drama

As a long-time scriptwriter, Suzanne Collins has spent a great deal more time writing dialogue than writing narrative. The switch to including descriptive passages was a challenge for her ("The Last Battle" by Rick Margolis, *School Library Journal* August 2010, pp. 24–27) because scripts are primarily dialogue and stage directions, while narrative contains a large amount of description.

To provide you with experience writing something other than narrative, this Writer's Forum is going to give you the opportunity to turn one of Collins's narrative passages into a dramatic scene from a play, teleplay, or screenplay.

A play, teleplay, or screenplay is a story told in speech. Except in unusual cases, the play script includes the words to be spoken and accompanying actions, but does not have the plot laid out to be told in narration the way a story (fiction) does. The playwright may give scene directions (tell briefly where set features, furniture, etc., are located and what they look like), but it is up to the production designer to fill in the missing details. Similarly, the playwright may give brief descriptions of the way the characters speak and move and interact, but it is up to the director and actors to fill in the missing details.

Plays consist mainly of dialogue, monologue, and asides—the words that the characters speak to one another, to themselves, and to the audience. So, although a play is very similar to a work of fiction in that it often has a protagonist, an antagonist, and a plot that includes an inciting incident, a confrontation, a climax, and a resolution, the difference is in the way those elements unfold for the audience.

Here is a sample of script format based on a passage from *Catching Fire* pp. 7–8. Notice how the narration is included in the dialogue or incorporated into stage directions, shown in italic type to differentiate them from words that are spoken by the actors.

(*Exterior Hazelle Hawthorne's house. Hazelle, looking out the window, sees Katniss approaching, carrying game bag.*)

HAZELLE. (*Opening door and ushering Katniss inside.*) Good morning, Katniss. Come in!

KATNISS. (*Removing game from bag onto the kitchen table.*) Thank you. Good haul today.

HAZELLE. (*Examining game, and picking up the beaver by its tail to feel its weight.*) He's going to make a great stew.

1. Use the information from *Catching Fire* pp. 11–12 and added facts that don't contradict anything that you've read so far in the trilogy to write a scene from a play in which the "genius" comes up with the idea to say that Gale is Katniss's cousin. Remember to stick to stage directions and dialogue to convey information.

Directions:
First, read the information. Then, answer the question or questions.

Catching Fire: A Teaching Guide 23

Chapter 3, page 30

Chapter 3 — The Victory Tour Begins

Vocabulary

tiger lily 30 a flower w/ orange petals
on the verge 30 almost at the point of
floods with 31 is tranformed by
depression 31 mental health issue combining sadness, inaction, loss of interests
incentive 33 something that will motivate
deception 33 act of deceiving
greenery 34 MM green parts of plants—leaves, stems, etc.
muted 34 (of sound) diminished
waterfowl 34 game birds that swim
tubers 34 underground fleshy stems that, in this case, serve as food
abreast of 35 up to date with
capricious 35 impulsive and unpredictable
mollify 36 calm; soothe
massages 36 rubs
incomprehensibly 37 to the point of being impossible to understand
resigns himself 37 accepts what cannot be altered
engrossed 38 absorbed; fully focused
readily 38 willingly
episode 38 incident
knack for 39 natural talent for
aspire to 40 hope to; have an ambition to
accommodate 40 do what is desired by
chirpy 40 cheerful and good-humored
encasing 41 surrounding
ermine 41 white winter fur of a weasel
expose 42 MM deprive of protection
halfhearted 42 w/out interest or warmth
crook 42 angle formed by bending the arm at the elbow
bidding ... goodbye 42 saying goodbye
indescribably 42 beyond description
voluminous 42 w/ great amounts of fabric
impact 44 effect

Journal and Discussion Questions

1. Evaluate Katniss's chances of success in carrying out her assigned mission.
2. How has Katniss's attitude towards her mother and stylists changed?
3. Read Yeats's poem "The Wild Swans at Coole" (http://www.poetryfoundation.org/poem/172060). Explain what Katniss and the speaker have in common.
4. What interpretation of the Capitol's influence on her future does Haymitch share with Katniss?
5. Summarize the chapter from Mrs. Everdeen's point of view.

Summary

Snow's proximity as he leaves allows Katniss to discern that his breath smells of blood, but not why. Reviewing Snow's mandate, Katniss thinks that Peeta would excel at it. She lies to protect her mother, saying the president visits all victors before the Tour. Her mother is relieved, and Katniss reflects on her belief that she will always have to protect her; Katniss's changed attitude towards her mother since the Games; finding a parallel between her current situation and her mother's depression after Mr. Everdeen's death; and—recollecting her mother's insistence to reporters that Katniss wasn't old enough to date—being spared from the pretend romance with Peeta for a few months.

As she bathes, Katniss decides that she should tell Haymitch about President Snow's visit. Her prep team bursts in and exclaims about the state of her eyebrows, nails, and hair. As they prep her, they say how lucky Katniss is to be a mentor in a Quarter Quell and predict Haymitch will draw attention because he won the last Quell, which Katniss can't remember seeing footage of. Mrs. Everdeen comes in to show the prep team how she braided Katniss's hair for the reaping. Then Katniss goes to find Cinna, with whom she's been planning her obligatory talent, clothes design, which is actually entirely done by Cinna. Peeta's talent, by contrast, is real, and it is painting. Effie Trinket arrives, and Prim comes home early from school, and her stance reminds Katniss of Rue.

Cinna helps Katniss into her coat, Mrs. Everdeen gives her the mockingjay pin for good luck, Effie shoves Katniss out the door, and Katniss resumes her madly-in-love act, breaking into a run, and falling to the ground in Peeta's embrace, knowing that he will be completely convincing for the cameras. On the train, Katniss waits till everyone is asleep and goes to find Haymitch. As the train stops for fuel, they go outside to be certain of not being overheard, and Katniss tells Haymitch about President Snow's visit and begs him to help her get through this trip. He disabuses her of the idea that it will be over after the trip—or ever, telling her that her only possible future is living happily ever after with Peeta in order to stay alive herself and keep her loved ones safe.

24 *Catching Fire: A Teaching Guide*

Strategy 7

Challenging the Status Quo

Directions: First, read the information. Then, answer the question or questions.

The mission President Snow assigns Katniss is to prevent uprisings. But why are uprisings a danger? One key reason may be that there are not any recognized avenues in Panem for legitimate political change.

One way to analyze a society is to examine the means it provides for political change and for challenging the status quo (the way things are). In the United States, there are a variety of means available, many of them set out in our Bill of Rights, the first ten amendments to our Constitution.

Amendment I—Congress shall make no law respecting an establishment of religion, or prohibiting the free exercise thereof; or abridging the freedom of speech, or of the press; or the right of the people peaceably to assemble, and to petition the Government for a redress of grievances.

Amendment II—A well regulated Militia, being necessary to the security of a free State, the right of the people to keep and bear Arms, shall not be infringed.

Amendment III—No Soldier shall, in time of peace be quartered in any house, without the consent of the Owner, nor in time of war, but in a manner to be prescribed by law.

Amendment IV—The right of the people to be secure in their persons, houses, papers, and effects, against unreasonable searches and seizures, shall not be violated, and no Warrants shall issue, but upon probable cause, supported by Oath or affirmation, and particularly describing the place to be searched, and the persons or things to be seized.

Amendment V—No person shall be held to answer for a capital, or otherwise infamous crime, unless on a presentment or indictment of a Grand Jury, except in cases arising in the land or naval forces, or in the Militia, when in actual service in time of War or public danger; nor shall any person be subject for the same offence to be twice put in jeopardy of life or limb; nor shall be compelled in any criminal case to be a witness against himself, nor be deprived of life, liberty, or property, without due process of law; nor shall private property be taken for public use, without just compensation.

Amendment VI—In all criminal prosecutions, the accused shall enjoy the right to a speedy and public trial, by an impartial jury of the State and district wherein the crime shall have been committed, which district shall have been previously ascertained by law, and to be informed of the nature and cause of the accusation; to be confronted with the witnesses against him; to have compulsory process for obtaining witnesses in his favor, and to have the Assistance of Counsel for his defence.

Amendment VII—In Suits at common law, where the value in controversy shall exceed twenty dollars, the right of trial by jury shall be preserved, and no fact tried by a jury, shall be otherwise re-examined in any Court of the United States, than according to the rules of the common law.

Amendment VIII—Excessive bail shall not be required, nor excessive fines imposed, nor cruel and unusual punishments inflicted.

Amendment IX—The enumeration in the Constitution, of certain rights, shall not be construed to deny or disparage others retained by the people.

Strategy 7, cont.

Amendment X—The powers not delegated to the United States by the Constitution, nor prohibited by it to the States, are reserved to the States respectively, or to the people.

When you are reading fiction, your own cultural, social, economic, and political situation—whatever they are—can serve as a jumping off point for analysis, because these are likely the systems that you know the most about. By comparing the culture, society, economics, and politics of your country (those that you are most familiar with) to what you find in a book, you can gain insight into the world of the book.

1. Make a list of the rights in the United States Bill of Rights that are not enjoyed by the citizens of Panem. Predict the effects that these differences would have on life in Panem. Then relate this state of affairs to the potential uprisings that President Snow has asked Katniss to prevent.

2. In an essay "Terrorism and the Uses of Terror" by Jeremy Waldron (*The Journal of Ethics*, 8: 5–35, 2004.), the author refers in a footnote to a proposal of a colleague, José Alvarez, and without quoting, says the following:

> "My colleague Jose Alvarez has suggested that a definition of 'terrorism' in terms of its characteristic aims may be fruitful if it identifies aims (or kinds of aim) that cannot be pursued using ordinary non-violent political means. For example: the modern world tries to put the boundaries and the basic legitimacy of most existing states beyond political question. Except in rare instances, political means are not defined for seeking revision of boundaries or revocations of basic legitimacy. So, political groups which pursue these ends are driven to adopt extraordinary means."

Write a paragraph in which you analyze how this quotation applies to Panem (or doesn't). Explain why you think as you do. If you find anything to critique in the quotation, explain your thoughts.

Chapter 4

Choosing Friendship; Arrival in District 11

Chapter 4, page 45

Vocabulary

slog 45 walk w/ difficulty, slowly and heavily
generates 45 gives rise to
blotting out 46 hiding from awareness
solitary confinement 46 imprisonment by oneself
beyond reproach 47 above all criticism
down 48 soft, short hairs
follicle 48 the small tube-shaped sac from which a human hair grows
scoured 48 washed with vigorous scrubbing
anointed 48 rubbed with oils and ointments (done in some religious ceremonies)
alterations 48 changes
implant 49 place in the body using surgery
talons 49 curved claws of a bird of prey (used figuratively on p. 381)
whims 49 sudden impulses
malfunctioned 49 failed to work properly
duplicitous 51 deceitful
descending 52 going down
recount 52 retell
entwined 52 interlaced; twisted together
lay it on thick 52 praise or apologize excessively
overkill 52 too much to be believable
breach 53 failure
etiquette 53 good manners
plague 53 afflict continually
standby 54 one that can be relied on (used ironically)
grazing 54 feeding on grasses and other plants at their leisure in a pasture
barbed wire 55 twisted wire with sharp points at close intervals
upscale 55 designed for people who are rich
preliminary 56 before the main event
vastness 56 very great size
facade 56 front wall of a building; architectural false front (often spelled façade)
sag 56 drooping
well-to-do 56 rich
verandah 56 a porch that is usually roofed and partially enclosed
good form 57 good manners
mildew 57 diseases caused by fungi, especially in damp conditions; also called *mold*
hunched 58 bent so as to cause a hump
luminous 58 shining
scripted 58 spoken exactly as written
precedent 59 earlier instance that provides a guide for the present
replica 59 imitation
passive 60 w/out taking action
mute 60 silent
allotted 60 amount allowed
pledged 60 promised
trace 60 hint
wizened 61 wrinkled (with age)
executed 61 carried out; done
spontaneous 61 done on the spot, without planning
elicited 62 brings out
defusing 62 literally, disarming an explosive device; figuratively, calming a dangerous situation
static 62 noise without meaning
acknowledge 62 show recognition of

Journal and Discussion Questions

1. Use the Choice Analysis Tool to compare Katniss's control of her romantic future with that of other inhabitants of District 12 and you, yourself.
2. What insight does Katniss gain into Haymitch through considering her own impending marriage?
3. If Katniss is correct in inferring that something was done to the young men in the arena to keep their beards from growing, what do you think was the intention?
4. What do you think Katniss would have done differently if she and Peeta had apologized and settled for friendship before the visit from President Snow?
5. What do you think the Capitol thinks of Peeta's talent?
6. List the differences Katniss and Peeta spot between District 12 and District 11. How do you account for these differences?
7. Besides the reasons Katniss offers, why else might their appearance in District 11 be in a confined area?
8. What do you think is the intended effect of placing the dead tributes' families on platforms in each district during the Victory Tour? How does this work out in District 11?
9. Katniss tries to think of something to say to undermine the effects of their presence in District 11. What do you think could accomplish this?
10. Summarize the chapter from Rue's reproachful sister's point of view.

Catching Fire: A Teaching Guide 27

Chapter 4 cont.

Summary

Back on the train, Haymitch tells Katniss she could do a lot worse (for a husband). Katniss lies in bed thinking that one of the few freedoms in District 12—the freedom to marry the person of one's choice or not marry—has been taken from her. She wonders if she will be forced to have children, and imagines that they would be forced into the arena, since the frequency with which victors' children have been chosen precludes chance. For the first time, she wonders if this is why Haymitch is alone and perpetually drunk. Trying to think of a way out, she again thinks of running away, but puts the thought aside till after the Victory Tour, during which she must focus on putting on the show required of her.

After a sleepless night, she is back in the hands of her prep team. The fact that Peeta gets to sleep late because men don't need as much prepping leads Katniss to reflect on the fact that none of the boys grew a beard in the arena and wonder what was done to them. As the prep team works, Flavius bemoans the fact that Cinna has forbidden any "alterations" to Katniss.

Growing more and more disconsolate, Katniss is first withdrawn, then snaps at Effie when the train has a breakdown, and leaves the train to go for a walk. Hearing footsteps behind her, she expects Haymitch, but it turns out to be Peeta, who has come to apologize for his behavior during the return from the Games. Katniss apologizes to him, but he says she was just keeping them alive and has nothing to apologize for. He suggests that they try "just being friends." Katniss agrees, feeling that this is more honest. She isn't prepared to tell Peeta what's really bothering her, so they start with the basics of friendship: favorite colors. They head back to the train to look at Peeta's paintings, and on the way, Katniss apologizes to Effie. Peeta's paintings turn out to be scenes from the Games, which he says he is able to capture so precisely because he sees them every night in his nightmares, which Katniss can relate to. He says he prefers to wake up with a paintbrush in his hand, rather than a knife, like Haymitch.

They go the observation car to look at District 11, and find an agricultural landscape enclosed with a thirty-five foot fence topped with barbed wire, guarded with watchtowers with armed guards. The vast size leads Katniss to wonder if there are preliminary drawings prior to the reaping. Arriving at the station, they find no welcoming committee, but a group of Peacekeepers who transport them in an armored car to the Justice Building for their public appearance.

As they take their places, Katniss wonders if she can work in a convincing kiss. Peeta gives a scripted response to the mayor's speech in their honor, and adds an unprecedented and unscripted offer of one month each year of the tributes' winnings to the District 11 tributes' families. Recalling Haymitch's comment about how she could do worse than Peeta and thinking that she couldn't do better, Katniss gets her kiss in. But as she goes to leave the platform, she catches sight of Rue's sister looking reproachful. Returning to the microphone, she thanks Rue and Thresh, paying her respects and thanking the families for their children and the entire community for the bread. As if on cue, an old man whistles Rue's four-note tune, and the entire community gives Katniss the District 12 salute. Katniss realizes that a public salute to a girl who defied the Capitol is not good, but as she tries to think of what to do, she hears her mic go dead. As Peeta goes back for the flowers she's left behind, she sees two Peacekeepers drag the whistler up the steps and shoot him in the head.

28 *Catching Fire: A Teaching Guide*

Strategy 8

Predicting and Recognizing Others' Perceptions

Predicting and recognizing characters' points of view is both an important skill for readers and a topic of this trilogy. Peeta points out the difficulty Katniss has in recognizing how others perceive her, telling Haymitch that Katniss doesn't understand the effect she can have on others (*HG* p. 91). Katniss continues to have difficulties making predictions about and recognizing how others perceive things in *Catching Fire*. It's a critical issue in her quest to fulfill the mission that President Snow gave her and in persuading others in order to accomplish her own plans. It's also a challenge to readers trying to "read through" her often inaccurate assessments, though Collins has constructed the narration to allow readers to see more than Katniss does. This makes it important to pay attention when our analysis of a character or situation differs from Katniss's: unreliable narrators always place more demands on the reader.

In real life, peoples' perceptions can be influenced by many factors that aren't necessarily obvious: their ethnic and cultural backgrounds, histories, education, work, preferences and biases, and beliefs. But in the real world, as we get to know them, we learn about these things. In Panem, district residents are purposely kept separate, interfering with their ability to gain this type of background knowledge about each other and intentionally hindering insight and communication.

Usually, those who are best at discerning others' viewpoints have broad knowledge and a certain maturity of understanding. So it is not surprising that Katniss—given her age and limited education—would not have a complete grasp of this, although she seems to be particularly lacking in this area when contrasted with, say, Peeta.

As we try to understand Peeta's comment and "read through" Katniss's deficiencies as an observer of others, we can look at four of the characterization elements in order to recognize both other characters' points of view and their perceptions of Katniss:

- **Words:** dialogue about the protagonist and how it is said—dialect, slang, and tone—are important; what is *not* said can also be important
- **Action:** what the character does with, for, or to the protagonist
- **Choices**: the decisions the character makes with regard to the protagonist
- **Change/Development:** the occurrence of and direction of change or development of interactions with the protagonist

1. Which characters show the greatest ability to predict and recognize others' perceptions?

2. As you continue reading, make a list of five characters who Katniss encounters for the first time in *Catching Fire* and write a brief summary of how each one perceives Katniss. Note that this is different from establishing their relationships, as we did in Strategy 3: Charting Character Development (p. 16). Also note any significant changes in the other characters' perceptions of Katniss.

3. For each character you chose to write about in 2, explain at least one way in which Katniss erred in her evaluation of him or her.

Directions:
First, read the information. Then, answer the question or questions.

Catching Fire: A Teaching Guide

Writer's Forum 2

Comparing/Contrasting Books in a Series

Unlike a stand-alone book, books in a series other than the first book have at least one volume of built-in material with which the author intends readers to compare and contrast the book they are reading. Key elements to consider for comparison and contrast include:

- events
- characters
- settings
- situations
- sequences
- relationships
- expressions of ideas, thoughts, and feelings

Comparing and contrasting material in a series is different from comparing or contrasting non-artistic things with some common feature(s)—say, train trips and cars trips—because the similarities and differences in artworks in a series arise from the artist's intentional action, whereas similarities and differences in other things created without such intention result from other types of factors. In the case of train and car trips, for example, factors include the design and engineering of cars and trains, the way their routes are planned as well as the beauty (or lack of beauty) in any particular route, the amenities offered (or not) for each type of travel, the distinctions (or not) in classes or service levels, the actual cost of operation, the number of personnel required for operation, etc. But car travel and train travel exist in their own rights: they don't exist in reference to each other, except for the person choosing between them for a particular trip, whereas books in a series intentionally exist in reference to each other.

Because the author of a series knows that readers will compare and contrast elements from different books, readers can count on the author having used repetitions to make meaning. If in two books in a series there seems to be repetition or contrast, it is almost always being used to communicate something—although what it is communicating is different in different cases.

1. Each item below points to a similarity between *The Hunger Games* and *Catching Fire*. Although it is not always fruitful to compare chapter by chapter, Collins's structure makes it interesting to do so in certain cases. Write a paragraph of comparison and contrast about each of the items. In each case, decide whether to use the point-by-point method or the block method, and incorporate words that signal comparison or contrast (see *The Hunger Games: A Teaching Guide* p. 32 to review comparison and contrast techniques). Identify the particulars of each case, examine how they are similar and different, and explain what meaning you can derive from each analysis.

    a. Chapter 1 of *The Hunger Games* and Chapter 1 of *Catching Fire* each have a scene of Katniss in the woods, anticipating an upcoming event.

    b. In Chapter 2 of *The Hunger Games* and *Catching Fire*, Katniss's life is suddenly at great risk.

    c. In Chapter 4 of *The Hunger Games* and *Catching Fire*, there's a significant change in Katniss's relationship with Peeta.

Directions:
First, read the information. Then, answer the question or questions.

Vocabulary

Chapter 5

Peeta Proposes; President Snow Is Not Satisfied

automatic weapons 63 firearms that can be fired continuously
encircles 63 goes around
lunatics 63 crazy people
backfired 63 MM had a harmless explosion in the exhaust system
ascend 64 climb
encounter 64 come upon
molding 64 strip of decorative material
cloying 64 so sweet as to cause disgust
maze 64 complicated network of paths
dome 64 vaulted roof
ledgers 64 books in which monetary transactions are recorded
grimy 64 dirty or sooty; filthy
in jeopardy 65 in danger of being harmed
exposed 65 MM uncovered through wear
springs 65 coils of wire designed to make furniture comfortable
inconsequential 65 unimportant
reliably 66 dependably; consistently
disrupt 66 interrupt; interfere with
overestimated 66 rated too highly
billows 67 rises in a great surge
hardships 67 sufferings
evoke 67 bring out; call forth
fury 67 extreme, violent anger
acutely 68 intensely
improbable 68 unlikely; unbelievable
ringlets 68 long spiral curls
barred 69 prevented from entering
architectural design 69 the set of values that architects use to plan buildings
ruins 69 remains of destroyed buildings
all the rage 69 fashionable
spontaneously 69 without forethought
validation 70 recognition; support
formation 70 set pattern of arrangements
dazzling 70 bright, shining
indistinguishable 71 unable to be perceived as separate and distinct
refineries 71 industrial plants where materials, such as petroleum, are purified
borderline 71 nearly
delirious 71 overcome with emotion
elation 71 joy
unruly 71 uncooperative
temporary insanity 72 a state of mental unbalance such that one cannot be held responsible for one's actions
frets 72 worries
haze 72 confused state of mind
discreet 72 careful, so as to avoid social embarrassment
besotted 73 overwhelmed
enfolding 74 enclosing
imperceptible 74 not able to be perceived

Journal and Discussion Questions

1. What are the descriptions of the hall and dome meant to evoke?
2. Why is Peeta angry?
3. At the end of Chapter 4, Katniss says that if she hadn't gone back for her flowers, they would have been "safe inside the Justice Building" and not seen the shooting. How would this have been altered what followed in Chapter 5?
4. What does Katniss learn about the Seventy-fourth Games that is new to her?
5. What inferences can you make about Effie and Portia from their exchange in this chapter?
6. How and why does Katniss's thinking about President Snow's assignment change?
7. Why does President Snow shake his head? What does this mean for Katniss?
8. Summarize the chapter from Effie's point of view.

Summary

As the whistler falls to the ground, Peacckeepers line up to block him from view and use their guns to push Katniss and Peeta inside. When they reach Haymitch, Effie, and the stylists, Peeta explains that a truck backfired. Haymitch hustles the victors into the dressing room—where he yanks off their mics and hides them under a cushion, and—despite his only having been in the building once, as far as Katniss knows—quickly guides them through a complicated route to the building's dome, where the layer of dust shows the lack of recent occupancy. Peeta responds to Haymitch's demand for what really happened and then asks Haymitch what's going on. Haymitch tells Katniss to fill Peeta in, so she details President Snow's visit and his orders for how she must behave on the tour. Peeta—realizing that his speech unwittingly made everything worse—knocks over a lamp and demands that Haymitch and Katniss stop hiding things from him, lest he unknowingly hurt the people he cares for. Haymitch explains that they didn't brief Peeta because he's so good about presenting himself, and Peeta counters that without information, he's likely to do damage. He asks about their "system" in the arena, and Katniss explains that she inferred what Haymitch was communicating from his gifts,

Chapter 5, cont.

and then realizes what this must have looked like from Peeta's perspective. Peeta says he knew Haymitch had to choose one tribute to support, and he's glad it was Katniss, but from now on, he needs to know what's going on. He angrily departs. Haymitch admits that since Peeta was determined to save Katniss, he chose her as the tribute he would try to bring home.

They leave the dome and prepare for the dinner in their honor, and Effie—who is not party to what happened—shares that her desire to look around the building was met with hostility by the Peacekeepers. As they wait to go in to the dinner, Peeta apologizes to Katniss, saying Haymitch has explained that Katniss was following his instructions and is not to blame and acknowledging that he, too, kept things from her in the past. They agree to be straight with each other, and Peeta asks if there was just one kiss with Gale.

This is the first of many dinners, train rides, and ceremonies, during which they now stick strictly to the script and try to assess their success in calming the districts, but feel that 8, 4, and 3 especially seem ready to explode. Katniss begins to have trouble sleeping and loses weight. Effie gives her pills to sleep that just lock her in her nightmares, so Peeta comes to comfort her, and sleeping in the same bed to forestall the nightmares becomes a habit. They are so desperate by the time they reach the Capitol that Katniss suggests a public wedding proposal. Peeta agrees but then disappears, and Haymitch explains that Peeta wanted it to be real, not part of strategy. Peeta proposes during their interview with Caesar Flickerman, and President Snow unexpectedly arrives to congratulate them. But when he embraces Katniss and she raises her eyebrows to ask if she succeeded, he gives his head a slight shake.

Strategy 9   Analyzing Assumptions

In analyzing the process of reading a series, we discussed that material from later books in a series may fulfill or subvert (undermine) reader expectations that were developed earlier in the series. Let's expand on this a bit. Controlling reader's expectations is an important part of all word crafting. In many genres of *non-fiction* writing and speaking, the author wants the audience to be aware of exactly what to expect from the very beginning. This is exemplified in the idea that in the introduction, one says what one is going to say; in the body, one says it; and in the conclusion, one reiterates what one said. In *fiction*, however, authors make use of suspense, and suspense is only possible if a) readers' expectations are sometimes not fulfilled and/or b) readers are surprised in other ways. Authors have a variety of means of shaping reader expectations and a variety of ways of creating surprise.

One way to control reader expectations is to have a character state an assumption in such a way that the reader accepts it as truth—whether the character presents it as fact, suggests that it's a fact, or acknowledges that it's an assumption. Other avenues are also available: a character can fail to state something that the author doesn't want known, or the narration can be constructed to de-emphasize elements that would lead the reader to figure out what's actually happening or is going to happen. In *HG* for example, stated assumptions led readers to expect that the odds matter, when in fact, many events went against the odds and in *CF,* it is suggested that the reaping lottery, for example, is a set-up. The appearance of the tribute–mutts chasing Cato, on the other hand, was a complete surprise.

With the choice to use first-person narration, the author has particular power to shape reader's expectations. If the narrator does not express something, there's no way for the reader to know. In addition, an *unreliable* narrator can have biases, make inaccurate assumptions, be in possession of inaccurate information, or misinterpret things. We have noted that Katniss has difficulty reading people, so she is likely to err—and mislead—often.

In Panem, there is another force at work. We cannot rely on what is said by authorities as being the truth. The fact that the powerful in Panem are not reliable is an added way to manipulate reader expectation. For example, we were led in *The Hunger Games* to assume that there could be only one victor, then two victors, then only one victor; then two victors were crowned.

All of these factors lead to a single conclusion: any time there's evidence of unreliability, readers should analyze stated assumptions carefully, and if the assumption doesn't ring true, see what conclusions can be drawn.

1. In Chapter 2, President Snow insists that Katniss turn things around on the Victory Tour, and Katniss assumes this is, in fact, possible. Evaluate this assumption.
2. In Chapter 3, Haymitch implies that Katniss has only one possible future. Analyze this assumption.
3. In Chapter 4, what assumptions did Peeta have about the purpose he and Katniss shared for the Victory Tour? Analyze this assumption from the perspective of Chapter 5.
4. In Chapter 5, what assumptions does Katniss make about Haymitch to explain his ability to navigate the Justice Building? Evaluate this assumption.

Directions: First, read the information. Then, answer the question or questions.

Strategy 10

Identifying Figures of Speech

The narration of *Catching Fire* has a much larger number of instances of figurative language than the narration of *The Hunger Games* did. Katniss most commonly uses three figures of speech: simile, metaphor, and personification.

- **Simile**: a comparison using words such as *like*, *as*, or *as if*.

"Like taking the lid off a pot and finding a fanged viper instead of stew." (p. 18)

Katniss uses a simile to compare the appearance of President Snow in an ordinary setting to finding a poisonous animal in one's dinner.

- **Metaphor**: a comparison in which two things that are, in fact, different are equated.

"They form a flock of small brown birds." (p. 58)

Katniss uses a metaphor to describe Rue's family.

- **Personification**: attributing thought or self-initiated action to inanimate objects.

"... the gold tattoos that used to be confined above her brows have curled around under her eyes ..." (p. 35)

Katniss uses personification to describe the change in Venia's appearance since she last saw her.

In order to understand the impact of figurative language, let's put each example up against a literal (not figurative) expression of the same thought (or as near as we can come).

- "Like taking the lid off a pot and finding a fanged viper instead of stew" — I met with an unexpected danger.
- "They form a flock of small brown birds." — Rue's sisters are small, graceful, and dark-skinned.
- "... the gold tattoos that used to be confined above her brows have curled around under her eyes ..."—Previously, she only had gold tattoos above her eyebrows, but now they have been extended, so that they curve around and under her eyes.

There are a number of ways we could describe the differences. We could say that the figurative language is more poetic, more colorful, more imaginative. When you find language of this type in the midst of prose, it's worth examining it to see if there are figures of speech, and if so, what this suggests about the narrator or character who is using them.

1. Find four metaphors and an instance of personification in Chapter 5. Write each figure of speech. Explain what Katniss is describing in each case.
2. Consider Katniss's use of figurative language overall. How does it affect your perception of her?

Directions: First, read the information. Then, answer the question or questions.

34   *Catching Fire: A Teaching Guide*

Chapter 6

The President's Party; Uprising in District 8

Vocabulary

catatonic 76 state of excessive excitement
mansion 76 house appropriate to a lord
exotic 77 coming from foreign places
mingle 77 move around a social gathering, greeting and chatting w/ various people
savory 77 pungent; pickled; salty; piquant
spirits 77 alcoholic beverages
puzzlement 77 confusion
frothy 78 foaming w/ little bubbles on top
embroidered 78 created w/ sewn patterns
intimate places 78 private parts
temptations 78 occasions of being lured
regimen 78 systematic process for control
abhorrent 78 hateful
ecstasy 79 overwhelming joy
stemmed 79 w/ a stem
detonate 79 blow up
sidetracked 81 deterred from one's plans
maggots 81 larva of flies
clandestine 83 secret
knockoff 83 copy or imitation
assortment 84 collection of different items
compulsive 84 w/ obsessive attention
punctuality 84 promptness
inebriated 84 drunk; intoxicated
down to a science 84 worked out to the last detail so as to get perfect results
immoral 86 morally wrong
wrenching 87 heart-breaking
gossipy 87 interested in discussing people's private lives and rumors about them
hustles 88 hurries
droning 88 making a continuous, unchanging humming sound
instinctively 88 w/out having to consider
hoarse 88 rough or grating
authoritative 88 official
textile 88 cloth, fabric

Journal and Discussion Questions

1. "Desperate diseases require desperate measures," is attributed to Guy Fawkes speaking to King James I on November 6, 1605. Look up Guy Fawkes, and explain how what you learn affects your understanding of Katniss's words (p. 75).
2. Why do you think Collins uses the image of children lying on a kitchen table?
3. What dangerous thought does Peeta voice? Why does he think this?
4. What does Katniss think of Plutarch? What do you think of her assumptions?
5. What do you think will result from the uprising in District 8?
6. Summarize the chapter from Plutarch Heavensbee's point of view.

Summary

Because President Snow's gesture means there's nothing more she can do to satisfy him, she feels freed. Thus, she is able to banter with President Snow when he suggests throwing her a wedding in the Capitol. The dinner in the Capitol is over-the-top, and Katniss sets out to taste everything, puzzling Peeta, who infers that they must have succeeded. Katniss notices that the mockingjay has become a fashion accessory. She quickly becomes full, and when her prep team explains and recommends the use of a vomit-inducing liquid in order to be able to eat more, both Peeta and Katniss are repulsed, and decide to dance, discussing the revolting use the Capitol makes of the districts, until Peeta suggests that perhaps they were wrong to try to diminish any possible uprisings, fortunately without appearing to be overheard. Portia interrupts to introduce the new Head Gamemaker, Plutarch Heavensbee, who requests a dance with Katniss. He mentions a meeting at midnight, takes out his pocket watch, and demonstrates that rubbing his thumb across the face makes a mockingjay appear and quickly vanish. He claims that it is one of a kind, and mentions that the meeting is meant to be secret, but he thought it would be safe to tell Katniss. Katniss dismisses the clandestine feel of the interchange as evidence of Plutarch's fear that someone will steal his watch idea.

Effie arrives to ensure they reach the train on time and sends them to bed almost immediately. For the first time in a long while, Katniss doesn't have nightmares, but she dreams of following a mockingjay, who is Rue, through the woods. Aware that they are almost home, Katniss thinks ahead to the dinner at Mayor Undersee's house and the Harvest Festival. This leads her to recollect how she and Madge became better friends after the games, so much so that Katniss has taken Madge into the woods. Katniss reflects that Madge doesn't see her parents much, her father being busy running District 12, and her mother suffering from intense headaches that often keep her bedridden. After Katniss is dressed for the dinner, she heads to Madge's room, stopping by the mayor's study to say hello. The study is empty, but the TV is on, and as she lingers—despite knowing better—Katniss sees footage showing an uprising in District 8, where all textile production has ceased.

Strategy 11
Understanding how Symbols and Motifs Are Developed

As we discussed in the teaching guide for *The Hunger Games* (Strategy 12: Understanding Symbolism and Motifs, p. 37), **symbolism** is a technique in which a person, place, thing, or idea represents not only itself, but also a deeper, more complex reality beyond itself. Symbols can work on different levels. There are universal symbols, national symbols, and cultural symbols, including religious and mythological symbols, for example. Many symbols involve allusion: you must know something else outside of the story to interpret the symbol. Symbols created by individual authors for particular books apply only in the context of a particular work or works.

We also discussed that **motif** is the name used for a significant, repeating element of a story. Folklorist Stith Thompson defined it as "the smallest element in a tale having a power to persist in tradition" (*The Folktale*, 1946, p. 415). Thompson defines the three classes into which most motifs fall as the *actors* in a tale, the *background elements*, and *single incidents*. A repeating element may be both a motif, if it is used in multiple works, and a symbol, if its use in a particular work is meant to call up things beyond its literal meaning.

Additionally, we determined in Strategy 11: Interpreting Names (p. 35) that **character names** and **place names** are used descriptively/symbolically in this trilogy. We saw that Katniss's name is symbolic, that people in the Capitol and Career districts have Latin names, and that names from certain districts come from nature or natural objects that are relevant to their district's industry.

In *CF*, Collins goes a step further, with two elements—fire and mockingjays, which begin to be explicitly discussed as symbolic, while their appearance in multiple books makes them motifs. You can look for these signals—repetition of elements in multiple books, patterns of names, and explicit discussion of items as symbolic—in other reading and treat them as an invitation to delve deeper into exploring different levels of meaning.

1. In *HG* and in the portion of *CF* you've read so far, assemble quotations and references that contribute to the growing perception of the symbolic meaning of mockingjays. Continue to collect material as you finish reading *CF*. Write a sentence summarizing your findings.

2. Build on your understanding of the symbolic meaning of fire in *HG* by explaining how its meaning is changing/growing in *CF*.

3. Continue your search for meaningful Latin names and names that come from nature. Identify character names in CF that follow these patterns and any meaning you can find that makes their names symbolic of who they are or what they do. Meaningful insights may come from different sources, and some names may not have clear meanings.

Nature
• *Hawthorne* – Hawthorn trees (*Craetaegus*) shelter and provide food for mammals and birds; the wood is very hard and resistant to rot—either fact could be understood figuratively.
• *Hazelle* – The hazel is a nut tree believed by the Celts to provide inspiration and wisdom.

Directions: First, read the information. Then, answer the question or questions.

Writer's Forum 3

Writing a Short Research Report

A short research report is a 3–5 page paper that reports the results of a well-organized investigation of a suitably narrow topic, casting light on it through the use of multiple, appropriate sources. Your task is to explore how the eating customs of Ancient Rome inform the president's party in Chapter 6. You will need to use *Catching Fire*, as well as authoritative sources that speak to culinary practices in Ancient Rome. Use your research as a basis from which to assess similarities and differences between food-related customs in Ancient Rome and the Capitol of Panem.

1. a. Reread Chapter 6. Write a preliminary thesis statement stating what you think the main idea of your paper will be. Your research may alter your main idea. That's fine: it's part of the process.

   b. Brainstorm the points of comparison that you will use, based on the elements of culinary practice that are covered in Chapter 6. List them. Write a short outline, using either the block form (discussing aspects of Roman culinary customs, then Capitol customs—or vice versa) or the point-by-point form (discussing each point in each of the two cultures before moving onto the next point).

   c. Locate sources of information. You may access **primary sources**—contemporary writings, either in Latin or translated—and **secondary sources**—an interpretation, evaluation, or critique of one or more primary sources. **Print sources** are those that have a physical existence on paper, such as books and journals; **digital sources** are computer files, and may also include books and journals, as well as images, multimedia, and works of art.

   d. In order to select which sources of information to use, you should evaluate them for appropriateness. These questions may help:
   - Is the source reliable and authoritative?
   - Is the source on-topic?
   - Is the source at a level that I can understand?

   You must choose a minimum of two sources besides *Catching Fire*, but not Wikipedia, because it is neither reliable nor authoritative. You may not use analysis of *The Hunger Games* trilogy that answers the question for you by having undertaken the same research. You may need to locate more than two sources in order to find two that meet the criteria. JSTOR and other databases, Google Books, and a reference librarian may be of value in locating sources.

   e. Take notes on your source, using your outline to organize your notes. Use **paraphrasing** (expressing the same thing in different words) and—as needed—short **quotations** and avoid **plagiarism** (unacknowledged use or overuse of someone else's words).

   f. Following your outline, use your notes to draft your paper, which should have an introduction that states your topic, a body, in which you provide the similar or contrasting information, and a conclusion, in which you review your points and derive what meaning you can. Be careful to use quotation marks to show others' words. Consider your teacher as your audience. Give your piece a title, when done.

   g. Create a bibliography in the style that your teacher suggests.

Directions: First, read the information. Then, answer the question or questions.

Chapter 7

Meeting Gale at the Lake to Plan an Escape

Vocabulary

spill my guts 90 tell all my secrets
grave 91 very serious; somber
composed 91 calmed
backfiring 91 MM having the reverse effect of what was intended
enhanced 91 improved
extinct 92 no longer existing
genetic code 92 patterns in DNA and RNA that form the biochemical basis of heredity
thrive 92 do well; prosper; flourish
excessive 92 beyond what is strictly necessary
conspicuously 92 noticeably
foundations 93 construction below the ground to support a building
woodpile 93 stack of logs assembled for burning later
obscure 93 hide
telltale 93 revealing
accumulated 93 collected
crouches 94 stoops with bent knees; squats
stunner 94 something that amazes
flexes 94 bends
that's optimistic 95 that's more hopeful than the situation warrants
uneasiness 95 insecurity; anxiety
dogged 95 followed
last-ditch effort 95 final, great effort to prevent a crisis
flask 95 a small bottle with a cap for carrying liquid
agitation 96 worry
all-too-familiar 97 so well known as to be completely predictable (usually of a sign of something unpleasant, annoying, or bad)
wilderness 98 region w/out people living in it or cultivated land; large area that is barren and undeveloped
reclaim 99 take back
backpedal 99 try to undo what's been said or done or its effects
untouchable 101 vile; loathsome; to be avoided at all costs
trudge 102 walk with heavy tread; plod
chapped 102 made rough or cracked by cold or wind
rueful 103 sad; sorrowful
twinge 103 sudden, sharp, momentary feeling—usually of pain, sorrow, guilt, or loss; pang

Journal and Discussion Questions

1. Explain the difference between Madge's and Katniss's understanding of the mockingjay.
2. When Gale says he guesses Katniss's plan is a "stunner," what do you think his tone is? Explain why you think as you do.
3. Why is Gale so happy about Katniss's plan to run away?
4. Why is Katniss's response to Gale's declaration of affection the "worst" she could have possibly made, in her opinion? Do you agree? Tell why or why not.
5. Whose interpretation of what Katniss has done to/for others do you think is correct: Gale's or Katniss's? Why?
6. Summarize the chapter from Gale's point of view.

Summary

The first Sunday after the Harvest Festival, Katniss heads to the woods to meet Gale, leaving markers to guide him to the lake because she no longer trusts that they will be unobserved in their old meeting place. As she travels, she recalls meeting the mayor in the hall outside his study, and after a friendly interchange, heading towards Madge's room, where she offered Madge the mockingjay pin back, and learned that it had belonged to Madge's aunt and was a family heirloom. She reflects that it's an odd choice of image because the invention of the jabberjays backfired on the Capitol, and even though Katniss outwardly agrees with Madge that mockingjays are not weapons, just songbirds, Katniss acknowledges in her thoughts that the mockingjays are a species that the Capitol didn't intend to come into existence.

When she reaches the lake, Katniss goes to the one remaining camp and lights a small fire. Gale arrives shortly carrying the items she'd left for him, and with a wild turkey carcass hanging from his belt and a bow on his shoulder. Katniss begins by telling him that President Snow threatened to kill him and she has a plan. She catches him up on key events since Haymitch's warning the night she and Peeta were crowned victors, while Gale prepares a meal for them. Gale interrupts and asks her to skip ahead to her plan, and she surprises him by suggesting they run away, actually making him happy, and leading him to embrace her and confess that he loves her. She responds, "I know," adding that he knows what he is to her and that she can't think about romance when she's so frightened. He breaks away in disappointment, but adds that they should run away and find out what she would feel under different circumstances. But when he finds out she wants to bring Haymitch and Peeta, he becomes angry. They argue, and Gale points out that President Snow can't afford to kill her or Peeta when he's planning their wedding, leading Katniss to reveal that there's an uprising in District 8, and immediately regret it. Gale takes the view that she's given people an opportunity and could do much to assist the rebellion, while Katniss argues that they have to leave before her actions kill more people. He departs alone, and as she heads back to the fence, Katniss determines to continue her escape plan, and talk to Peeta next.

Katniss runs into Peeta at the edge of the Victor's Village, and falls in with him as he heads to town to dine with his family. When she blurts out her idea, he takes her arm and responds that whether he'd join her depends on why. She tells him that President Snow wasn't convinced, and there's an uprising in District 8. He asks who else is involved, and when he asks about Gale, Katniss admits Gale might have other plans. Peeta says he'll come, but adds that he doesn't believe she'll go, leading Katniss to angrily pull her arm away from him. He suggests checking with Haymitch to ensure they won't make things worse, and then notices a commotion in the town square. As soon as they get close, Peeta blocks Katniss and begs her in a low tone to go home, promising to join her soon. Katniss ignores him and pushes though the gathered people, who also attempt to push her back and keep her from reaching whatever is going on. When she arrives at the front of the crowd, she sees why: Gale is bound to a post by his wrists, with the wild turkey hanging above him and a man—not Cray—in the Head Peacekeeper's outfit whipping him.

Chapter 7, cont.

Catching Fire: A Teaching Guide 39

Strategy 12

Understanding Complex Motivations

In the teaching guide for *The Hunger Games*, we discussed that **character traits** are often spoken of as absolutes, when they are better considered as ranges. Motivations, too, may be more complex than they first appear.

In short stories or standalone works of fiction, characters may have simple, straightforward motivations that fit well with the length and relative simplicity of the story. But in series with character development, the length can make it possible and desirable to add the complexity of mixed motivations. And when characters are being coerced or terrorized—as most citizens of Panem are—there will always be two layers of motivation: what the character really wants and what he or she is forced to seek by the controlling circumstances. These two layers of motivation are often, but not always, opposed and often, the personal motivation may give way to coercion or terror, but not always. Let's look at the possibilities more carefully.

The first, and most typical, situation is characters who suffer an internal conflict between what they want and what they are being forced to do, which makes sense because why would force or threats be used except to overcome something? In unusual cases, a character may, at least briefly, be in a situation in which his or her internal, personal desires match what he or she is being coerced or terrorized into doing, so that's a second possibility. Usually in this case, there is some striking difference to offset the match. Third, there are characters who don't experience conflict because they simply refuse to be coerced or terrorized and are ready to fight to the death to resist. Fourth, there are those who become willing tools of the terrorizing or coercing person or entity, oblivious to what they are engaged in. Fifth and finally, there are those who use apparent cooperation to mask their efforts to undermine the terrorizing or coercing person or entity they seem to serve.

When you read dystopias and other works in which oppression or other forms of control are exerted over an individual or population, look for these various expressions of complex motivations.

1. Name at least two characters who suffer an internal conflict caused by the tension between what they want and what they are being forced to do through coercion or terrorizing. Explain your reasoning for your categorization of each.
2. Name at least one character who has a simple and straightforward motivation that fits—at least temporarily—with what he or she is being coerced or terrorized into doing. Explain your reasoning for your categorization.
3. Name at least two characters who simply refuse to be coerced or terrorized, and are ready to fight to the death to resist. Explain your reasoning for your categorization of each.
4. Name at least two characters who seem to be oblivious tools of the Capitol regime. Explain your reasoning for your categorization of each.
5. The trilogy has not directly stated that there is any character who is using apparent cooperation with the terrorizing person or entity as a cover for attempts to undermine it. Explain any suspicions you have about any character(s) who may fit this description. Provide evidence that supports your suspicions.

Directions:
First, read the information. Then, answer the question or questions.

Chapter 8 — The Whipping

Vocabulary

welt 106 raised ridge on the skin
pupils 106 holes where light enters eyes
camera ready 107 sufficiently beautiful
detect 107 identify the existence of
repercussions 108 payback; consequences
dispensed 108 given out; administered
compassion 109 sympathy for others' suffering
visibility 111 the ability to see
curt 111 abrupt; so brief as to be rude
immune to 111 untouched by
sterile 111 clean and free from germs
tinctures 111 solutions of medicine in alcohol
tapered 111 long, slender, and narrowing at one end
in(to the) zone 113 in a state of focused attention that enhances performance
resonate 113 evoke a shared feeling
slit 114 long, but very narrow, opening
vying 114 contending; competing
vials 115 small, capped containers
nettles 116 annoys; irritates
deflate 116 become less on edge
stubble 116 bristly growth of whiskers between one shaving and the next
phantom 117 imaginary
shunned 118 treated as an outcast
defy 118 act against the interests of
opiates 118 drugs to relieve pain and induce sleep
quarry 119 hunted animals; prey

Journal and Discussion Questions

1. Compare and contrast Darius's, Haymitch's, Katniss's, and Purnia's responses to Romulus Thread's actions.
2. Multiple times in *Catching Fire* (e.g., pp. 18, 83, and 107), Katniss asks herself a question and answers it. Assess what Collins achieves with this technique.
3. Use the Choice Analysis Tool to evaluate Katniss's comments on her motivations on p. 118 in *CF*. Then compare/contrast with what she says in *HG*, pp. 358.
4. Which amendments in the Bill of Rights does Romulus Thread violate? Explain.
5. Make a line graph of Katniss's emotional state through the chapter. Label it.

Summary

Katniss springs forward to stop the next blow and catches the lash on her left cheek. She is screaming at the Peacekeeper when Haymitch interrupts, stepping over Darius—who lies unconscious on the ground, to reach Katniss. Speaking as mentor, he asks rhetorically what he's supposed to tell Katniss's stylist about the wedding shoot next week, to which the whip wielder, whose accent makes it clear that he's from another district, responds that Katniss interrupted punishment of a "confessed criminal," and her cheek is not his problem. Haymitch responds that it will be when he calls the Capitol. Peeta joins them in blocking the Peacekeeper from reaching Gale. At this point, a member of the backup Peacekeeping squad, which is still composed of locals, indicates respectfully that the required punishment for a first offense has been fulfilled. The new Head acquiesces, tells Katniss to get her cousin away, and warns that the next offense will mean the firing squad. As the crowd disperses in fear, a couple of Gales coworkers help carry him to Mrs. Everdeen, while a former neighbor of Katniss's goes to tell Hazelle. Heading to the Victor's Village, the group puts together the likely sequence of events: Gale took the wild turkey to Cray's house, as usual, only to discover there was a new Head Peacekeeper, Romulus Thread. Thread began the punishment, and Darius tried to intervene after 20 lashes of 40 total, but was disrespectful.

Gale is laid on the Everdeen's kitchen table, and Mrs. Everdeen and Prim launch into action, while Peeta holds a cloth with snow to Katniss's cheek. Katniss questions her mother's use of painkillers that she considers too mild, and Haymitch and Peeta carry her out of the room and pin her to a bed while she shrieks obscenities at her mother. When she's done with Gale, Mrs. Everdeen comes in and treats Katniss's cheek. The doorbell rings, making Katniss jump, fearing Peacekeepers, but it's Madge, bringing some of her mother's pain medication for her headaches—morphling, from the Capitol. Katniss goes to sit with Gale and imagining their situations reversed, considers the hatred she'd feel for the girl whom he had promised to marry to win the Hunger Games, and feels that they belong to each other. As she reconsiders her actions to win the Games and her mixed motivations, she is filled with self-loathing. She wonders if others are right in assessing her trick with the berries as an act of rebellion, and concludes that life in District 12 is not so different from life in the arena. She kisses Gale, who wakes for a moment and says he thought she'd be gone. But she affirms that she's going to stay and make all kinds of trouble, and he says he will, too, before losing consciousness again.

Writer's Forum 4

Writing Up an Investigation

Often when we analyze, we are able to use established categories, a standard on which to base our evaluation. For example, classroom teachers often give students a rubric to clarify how the teacher will analyze their work. Because teachers choose their assignments to showcase what they wish to assess (for example, structuring an argument, creating a Works Cited list), the categories are clear. We're going to look at a case in which there are no established categories: the question of how to create a good character without making the character unbelievably or annoyingly good—a *goody two-shoes*. Let's start be defining the term.

In 1765, a children's book called *The History of Little Goody Two-Shoes* was published by John Newberry of London. It told a Cinderella-type story of an orphan named Margery Meanwell—the character referenced by the title—who begins the story so poor that she only has a single shoe. She works hard, is educated, does well for herself, and marries a well-to-do widower, demonstrating that virtue is rewarded. Originally, the epithet *goody two-shoes* referred to this virtuous and nearly perfect character. In the 1930s, though, the usage changed, with the term coming to be used to mock those whose virtue was so continuous that it seems to be on display, rather than done for the sake of the good—making everyone's efforts seem inadequate. It can also refer to someone who seems just too good to be true or a hypocrite, who successfully conceals his or her failings with the appearance of goodness. As you read, watch for ways good characters are kept from being "too good."

1. Any very good character can lean towards being a *goody two-shoes*. How can this pitfall be avoided? You're going to answer this question by studying two characters in this trilogy: Prim and Peeta. Both are good, but each avoids being a *goody two-shoes*. How does Collins do this? We can start by establishing some categories for what makes a character good, but you're going to have to investigate to find approaches, material, and techniques that somehow balance these characters' goodness and choose category labels for them.

   a. Using prior knowledge and/or research (e.g., rereading parts of the trilogy), write an introductory paragraph that tells the purpose of the paper and defines a set of categories for "good behavior." For example, one category might be 'appropriately apologetic' after doing wrong.

   b. Review the *The Hunger Games* and *Catching Fire* (up to Chapter 8) to find scenes in which Prim and Peeta appear or are mentioned. Write a paragraph that describes what makes each of the two characters good: which categories of goodness do they exhibit?

   c. Now, examine how—in *The Hunger Games* and *Catching Fire*—Collins uses approaches, material, and/or techniques to create balance for each of these characters and prevents each of them from becoming a *goody two-shoes*. Look especially for repeated approaches that you can categorize. Write a paragraph describing these categories (keeping in mind that other authors may use other means).

   d. Write one or two paragraphs in which you use your categories to discuss how Collins balances out the Peeta's and Prim's goodness.

   e. Write a conclusion that pulls it all together and evaluates Collins's success in using the techniques and approaches she chose to employ.

Directions: First, read the information. Then, answer the question or questions.

Chapter 9

Katniss Plans an Uprising; Second Trip to the Lake

Chapter 9 Page 120

Vocabulary

throbs 120 beats like the heart
elongating 121 extending
snout 121 long, projecting nose and jaws of an animal; muzzle
strangled cry 121 choked off cry
blizzard 121 violent snowstorm
retaliation 122 revenge; payback
lurking 122 present w/out attracting notice
distintegrates 122 falls apart; collapses
justification 123 acceptability based on a reason or principle
crucial 123 all-important; critical; absolutely necessary
impotent 124 powerless
catalyst 124 agent of change
unflinching 124 rock solid; unable to be swayed or lessened
tongue-tied 124 at loss for words
tending 124 taking care of
ladle 124 serve w/ a long-handled, deep-bowled spoon
tormented 124 feeling great physical pain
tepid 125 lukewarm
numbs 125 stops feeling
remorse 125 regret and moral pain; guilt
drifts 127 piles of snow created by blowing
out of earshot 128 too far away to hear
pristine 128 pure; perfectly clean
cobblestones 128 rounded paving stones
whipping post 128 wooden post to which offenders are tied for whipping
stockades 128 barriers built for defense
gallows 128 devices on which to carry out executions by hanging

rubbing alcohol 129 poisonous solution applied externally in medical treatment
inherent 130 built-in; inseparable
thwarting 130 opposing; defeating
stroll 131 leisurely walk, often w/out a goal
blatantly 131 obviously; clearly
defiled 132 made filthy; damaged so as to be unclean and unusable
installations 132 building projects
resolve 132 commitment; determination
standard of living 132 quality of and level of comfort in living situation
stocks 132 heavy wooden devices to hold people by ankles, and sometimes by wrists as well, for public punishment
gaunt 133 thin, tired-looking; worn from tiredness and hunger
omnipresent 133 ongoing; never-ending
insulated 133 lined w/ material to prevent heat from escaping
recreational 133 having to do with exercise and pleasure (rather than official duties)
thermal 133 designed to retain heat
slinking 133 sneaking; moving so as to avoid notice
pockmarked 133 w/ small pits in its surface
glare 134 bright, blinding light
indentations 134 hollowed out spots
iris 134 the colored portion of the eye, within which the pupil sits
waver 134 become less certain or unsure
incriminating 135 revealing the guilt of

Journal and Discussion Questions

1. Read the section of Katniss's reflections on p. 121 from "I wish that Peeta were . . . " to the end of the paragraph. What conclusions do you draw about Katniss's feelings, state of mind, and perceptions in light of her complex motivations?

2. On p. 123, Katniss makes the "crucial first step" of deciding not to run away. Use this development to reflect on Gale's (p. 100) and Peeta's (p. 103) responses to her proposal to run away. What light is shed on the two men's understandings of Katniss?

3. Review Katniss's feelings when remembering 1) Gale kissing her at the fence (27–29); 2) her kissing Gale in her kitchen (pp. 125–6). Explain why she feels as she does in each case.

4. A *straw man* is a technique in which a weak argument is set up only so it can be refuted. How does Collins use a similar technique in this chapter?

5. Do you agree with Haymitch's assessment of Katniss's ability to start an uprising? Explain why you think as you do, using evidence to support your opinion.

6. What conclusions do you draw from Katniss's and Peeta's reactions to Haymitch's announcement that he's going to see if he can get some rubbing alcohol?

7. Explain who you think is facing Katniss (p. 134) and what you think her plans and goals are, based on the available evidence up to the end of Chapter 9.

8 Summarize all the changes in this chapter made by Romulus Thread in his administration of District 12 "peacekeeping."

Catching Fire: A Teaching Guide 43

Chapter 9, cont.

Summary

Peeta awakens Katniss, who has fallen asleep in the kitchen, holding Gale's hand. Peeta has brought fresh bread and appears to have been up all night. Remembering how he helped her protect Gale and his willingness to run away with her, she starts to speak, but he cuts her off, urging her to sleep. When she does, she dreams variations of events from the Hunger Games melded with her new injury. She wishes for Peeta before recalling that she's chosen Gale, and thinking that a future with Peeta is part of the Capitol's design for her, not her choice for herself. Noticing a blizzard starting, Katniss welcomes it as an opportunity to plan. She explicitly acknowledges the likely outcomes of choosing to stay and fight: arrest, torture, and death for herself and her family and friends. Her resolve is shaken when she thinks of Prim until she considers what the Capitol has already done to her. She decides Gale was right about this being an opportunity, and as she showers, she contemplates how the uprising in District 8 was organized, if it was organized, and how it could be replicated in District 12. She doesn't see herself as a catalyst for rebellion, being too tongue-tied, but thinks that Peeta's way with words would be ideal.

She goes downstairs to find her mother and Prim treating Gale with a mixture of snow and herbs called *snow coat*, which gives him notable relief, and her mother gives Katniss a pack for her cheek. Katniss apologizes for her outburst, and her mother tells Katniss that she's seen how people react when a loved one is in pain, and while Katniss does think she loves Gale in some way, she's not sure either in what way or which way her mother means. Finding that Peeta's gone home. Katniss calls him, and he suggests they won't be able to talk until the blizzard is over. When it stops snowing, Katniss, Peeta, and Haymitch head to town, waiting to get out of the Victor's Village before Haymitch asks about Katniss's plan to run away, and she says she wants to start an uprising, which just makes him laugh before telling her it won't work. When they reach the square, they find it transformed, with a large banner of the seal of Panem, machine gun nests on the rooftops, and a newly constructed whipping post and gallows in the center. A blaze a few blocks away marks the destruction of the Hob. Peeta goes with Katniss to check on Hazelle, who hasn't been by since the snow was cleared. As they walk, Katniss analyzes what she sees as a key flaw in her uprising plan: the people of District 12 were scared to go to the Hob, let alone explicitly defy authority.

It turns out Hazelle stayed home because her daughter has the measles. She tells them that the mines are closed till further notice and she's lost all her laundry customers, who are afraid of being connected with her now. Katniss gives her a pile of money, and heads for the Hob, and Peeta insists on accompanying her and dissuades her from checking on Greasy Sae. They stop by the bakery, and as they head home, Katniss notices that she doesn't recognize any of the Peacekeepers.

Over the next days, people begin to suffer from the loss of mine income, more and more children are signing up for tesserae, and food shortages set in. The mines finally reopen, but with wages cut and hours lengthened, and miners are sent to work in the most dangerous sections. The Parcel Day food arrives, but it is spoiled. And many people are punished in the square. Mrs. Everdeen is getting so many patients that her remedy supplies are running out. Gale gets well enough to go home, but only after his brother Rory has signed up for tesserae, though Katniss gets Haymitch to hire Hazelle as a housekeeper. Katniss and Gale strictly avoid the woods until a crate of wedding dresses arrives, and Katniss—feeling that she has to have a few hours of freedom—heads to the lake, so preoccupied, that she doesn't notice the signs that others are present until she hears a weapon cocked behind her. Turning and drawing an arrow, Katniss sees a Peacekeeper uniform, but immediately the woman drops her weapon, cries out for Katniss to stop, and holds something out to her. Katniss is reluctant to lower her defenses until she sees that the cracker the woman is holding is stamped with the image of a mockingjay.

Strategy 13

Understanding Parallels and Repetition

In a series, there is often repetition of information, and we've already discussed the role of recapping material from previous books at the start of each new book in a series. But not all repeated information occurs in this location. Material repeated in other locations may have a purpose other than to reprise the main characters and events from the previous volume(s).

Authors may also build meaning by creating parallels in characters, events, and structure. We've already remarked on the fact that Collins has created a trilogy of books and divided each of the books into three equal parts, laying out a very clear three-act structure. You have now completed the first third of *Catching Fire*, putting you in the position to begin making structural comparisons between the first two books of *The Hunger Games* trilogy.

Repetition of facts can point to the importance of what is repeated. Repetition of events and parallels both can add a layer of meaning for readers who catch the tip-off and use it to think back to (or check back with) the earlier material. They can also invite the reader to note progressions and draw contrasts, noting not only what is similar but what is different and/or changed with time. Rowling's setting of each Harry Potter book over the course of a school year showed progress in this way, and parallels and repetitions are worth examining in any series. Let's take this opportunity to analyze some of the important/outstanding repetitions and parallels that have occurred between the first two books of the Hunger Games trilogy so far.

Information

1. Read the passage in *The Hunger Games* p. 42–3 about mockingjays and jabberjays and the passage in *Catching Fire* pp. 91–92. Identify and explain the purpose of their similarities and differences.

Characters

2. What do you make of the parallels that cause Katniss to link Rue and Prim?

3. As he retells it in *The Hunger Games* Peeta, having heard the story of his father falling in love with Katniss's mother, falls in love with Katniss (pp. 300–301). What do you make of this parallel?

Events

4. Chapter 4 in both of the first two books in the trilogy involves a train trip to a new place. Examine the parallel for what it reveals.

5. When Peeta and Katniss approach the square in Chapter 7, Peeta begs her to leave. What incident in *The Hunger Games* does this parallel. Examine the parallel for what it reveals.

Structure

6. In a series, the inciting incident for books after the first has a different role than the initial inciting incident in the first book. Nevertheless, comparing them can be fruitful. Compare and contrast the inciting incidents in *The Hunger Games* and *Catching Fire*.

7. Identify the first plot point or reversal in *The Hunger Games* and *Catching Fire*. How can they be seen as a progression? What does this suggest will happen in the remainder of the trilogy?

Directions: First, read the information. Then, answer the question or questions.

Test: Chapters 1–9

Vocabulary

Look at each group of words. Tell why it is important in the story.

1. black market, stockpiling, white liquor, stall
2. facade, verandah, dome
3. clandestine, one-of-a-kind, knockoff
4. extinct, genetic code, thrive
5. backpedal, defuse, untouchable
6. sterile, remedies, tinctures, vial, opiates
7. whipping post, stockades, gallows
8. architectural detail, ruins, all the rage

Essay Topics

1. What evidence in Part I suggests that the Capitol intends that—although there is time between Games and the numbers change—the Games are never, ever really over?

2. How does the new information about the participation of District 12 in the Seventy-fourth Hunger Games affect your view of the Games?

3. What does Katniss mean when she questions whether any of her kisses with Peeta "counted" (p. 27)? Do you think they counted? Explain why you think as you do.

4. Chart the discussion of running away in the trilogy so far.

5. Analyze the use of sensory detail in the paragraph about the lake (pp. 33–34).

6. Analyze Panem's definition of *talent* (p. 39) by comparing it to the word *hobby* and to its dictionary definition. How do you think people around Panem are likely to respond to Katniss's and Peeta's talents and why?

7. Does Haymitch believes Katniss can fulfill President Snow's mission (p. 43)? If he does, why isn't he more supportive? If he doesn't, why does he say what he does?

8. What light do Katniss's conclusions about the situations in districts outside of District 12 (pp. 67–68, 71) shed on possible motives for President Snow's visit?

9. What is Katniss's motivation for dissuading Gale from starting an uprising? Explain.

10. What is your interpretation of the fact that someone outside of District 12 has a cracker with a mockingjay and, lowering a weapon, shows it to Katniss while begging not to be shot?

11. If you were the author of this story, what would happen next? How would you develop the plot.

Chapter 10

PART II "THE QUELL"
Bonnie and Twill

Chapter 10, page 139

Vocabulary

renderings 139 interpretations
fashion statement 139 attire intended to show one's taste and awareness of style
imminent 139 about to happen
strawberry birthmark 140 raised, red birthmark, technically a *hemangioma*
fluke 141 unpredictable chance
translucent 142 almost see-through
urban 142 located within a city
fumes 142 vapors caused by chemical reactions
tenements 142 poorly tended, overcrowded apartment buildings
quaver 142 shaking
malnourished 142 underfed
din 144 constant loud noise
dock 144 platform for loading cargo
granary 144 storage building for threshed grain
armory 144 storage building for arms
undying 144 never-ending
sheer 145 apart from anything else (used of the key factor)
overthrow 145 removal from power; defeat
lockdown 145 confining citizens so the authorities can regain control
brink 145 edge
impassable 145 unable to be crossed
outskirts 146 outer edges
footage 146 videotape
nuclear development 147 development of power sources or weapons that use the energy from atomic nuclei through fission or fusion
graphite 147 form of carbon used in nuclear reactors
justify 147 provide sufficient reason for
delusions 148 fantasies
assimilating into 148 becoming part of
insubstantial 148 lacking substance
solar energy 148 energy from the sun
tantalizing 149 tempting; very desirable
derailed 149 halted; stopped
momentum 149 force of forward motion
ploy 150 a strategic move
inflammatory 150 arousing strong feelings; inciting
unwittingly 150 w/out knowing it
innocuous 150 harmless

Journal and Discussion Questions

1. What do you think it means to "be on [Katniss's] side" (p. 139)?
2. How do you interpret the parallel between the two sets of escapees whom Katniss has met in the woods outside District 12?
3. How do you interpret the parallel implicit in Katniss's comparison of Bonnie and Rue?
4. Collins chooses to have Katniss retell/summarize Bonnie's and Twill's story, rather than allowing us to listen to their rendition along with Katniss. Why do you think she made this decision? Provide evidence to support your conclusion, if possible.
5. Compare and contrast the Capitol's response in District 12 as Romulus Thread settled in with the response to the attempted uprising in District 8.
6. What about her interaction with Bonnie and Twill casts Katniss's visit with President Snow in a new light for Katniss?
7. Assess Katniss's surmise about the role of her wedding (p. 150).
8. What does the fact that the electrified fence has been turned on indicate to you? Explain why you think as you do.
9. Predict how Katniss will get back to District 12.
10. Summarize the chapter from Twill's or Bonnie's point of view.

Summary

While Katniss can see that the mockingjay on the cracker is not a fashion statement, like those in the Capitol, she doesn't know what it means. A voice behind her explains that it's showing their affiliation with Katniss's cause, and Katniss orders the speaker to come in front of her. As soon as she sees her, Katniss knows she's not a Peacekeeper or Capitol citizen, and that she's injured. Katniss demands their identities, and the first woman, who is older, identifies herself as Twill and the younger woman with the limp as Bonnie. They've escaped from District 8, and Twill explains that they're heading for District 13. Katniss says out that 13 was destroyed, but Twill points out the destruction took place 75 years previously. Katniss has the sense that they're telling the truth, but—recalling the red-headed Avox—asks if they're being followed. Twill responds that they're believed to be dead. They move to the lake house, where there is a half-hearted fire and

Catching Fire: A Teaching Guide 47

Chapter 10, cont.

some pine needles brewing for tea. Recalling that District 8 is urban, so its denizens would not have experience in the woods, Katniss is not surprised to hear they're out of food, and since her game bag is full—albeit as a subterfuge to suggest to her mother that she's out feeding the hungry in District 12—she feeds them cheese buns and asks for their history.

They tell her that discontent had been growing since the Hunger Games, and the loud machinery in the textile factories served to cover whispered conversations to plan the uprising. Twill taught school, and Bonnie was her student, but both worked in the factory after school. Bonnie, who worked on the loading dock, had collected the uniforms, intended to help Twill and her husband get to other districts to spread the word of the uprising. They used the Victory Tour as a rehearsal, since the target was to take over the key buildings in the square. The night of the engagement was the night they put their plan into action, since it was mandatory viewing and provided an excuse to be out after dark. At 8 p.m., they donned masks and set upon the Peacekeepers, hoping that they could get word out so it wouldn't be an isolated incident. But thousands of additional Peacekeepers were flown in, hovercrafts bombed the rebels, and within 48 hours, the city was subdued and put on lockdown for a week, with no food or coal. Then there was an order to return to work. Bonnie and Twill were late getting to the factory after school because the bombs had blocked the streets, and that is why they weren't there when the was factory exploded—likely as retribution for being the site of the planning—killing all present, including Bonnie's whole family and Twill's husband.

Figuring they were assumed dead, the two women got the Peacekeeper uniforms, stole food from their dead neighbors, and hopped a boxcar of fabric on a train to District 6. From there, they continued on foot, using the train tracks as a guide. Twill explains that they'd spotted that the Capitol keeps reusing the same footage of District 13 with the same mockingjay in the upper right-hand corner, leading them to conclude that what is actually there cannot safely be shown. Twill believes the people moved underground and that the Capitol doesn't interfere because District 13's industry was nuclear development. Katniss protests that they were graphite miners, but realizes that the Capitol is the source of that information, and then demands why residents of District 13 haven't helped the other districts, if they're there. She concludes that the women are deluded, but she gives them all the food in her bag, tries to teach Twill some basics of hunting, and shows Bonnie how to properly build a fire. They ask her for information about District 12, and she shares the facts of the new regime. They are deeply moved as they embrace Katniss, but she is dismissive and heads back towards the fence, preoccupied with the idea that President Snow's visit was aimed at focusing her attention on her behavior so she wouldn't do anything else to spur uprisings. Just before reaching the fence, she realizes she didn't get the story behind the cracker, and wonders if she unintentionally has become the face of the rebellion. She hides her weapons, and approaches the fence, realizing only just in time that it has been activated.

Strategy 14 Understanding Shockers

As we discussed in the teaching guide for *The Hunger Games*, a cliffhanger is a way of handling the temporary ending in a narrative that is going to be continued. A cliffhanger generally leaves the protagonist or another major character in peril or provides (or hints at) a major revelation. All will be revealed . . . but not until after the break.

This narrative strategy helps build suspense. It makes the audience long for the next portion and encourages them to think about the story even when they're not actively engaged with it.

But there are some temporary endings that include a revelation for which the reader's first thought is not "I wonder what's going to happen next?" but "I can't believe it!" Let's distinguish these from classic cliffhangers by calling them *shockers*. It is useful to distinguish a shocker from a classic cliffhanger because a classic cliffhanger creates a sense of urgency, immediately leading the reader to look ahead. The shocker, on the other hand either keeps the reader in the here-and-now for at least awhile, pondering the unexpected reversal or surprise and its implications, or it encourages the reader to look back to try to understand if the development makes sense in terms of what came before or if clues that pointed to it were missed. It is important to note that whether a temporary ending is interpreted as a classic cliffhanger or a shocker may rely partly on the particular reader as well as the words provided by the writer.

Here's an example of a temporary ending that may be classified as a shocker. At the end of Chapter 1 of *Catching Fire*, we learn that President Snow is not only in District 12: he is in Katniss's home! Readers may first just be startled and then stop and consider how and why President Snow has come to the Everdeen's home and whether they should have anticipated this development before moving on to consider what he is likely to say or do to Katniss in the next chapter. So, depending on which way the reader's reactions tend, this could well be a shocker, as well as a cliffhanger.

When you read or view works that have temporary endings, when you reach each one—whether it's a commercial break or a chapter break—it can help you understand the experience the creator is hoping for you to have by classifying the ending as classic cliffhanger, shocker, or other.

1. For Chapters 2–10, identify and describe the classic cliffhangers and shockers you find. Then describe any endings that function differently, by, for example, rounding out an incident or inviting a review of what went before.

Directions:
First, read the information. Then, answer the question or questions.

Chapter 11
Page 172

Chapter 11

The Electrified Fence; The Family Book

Vocabulary

strand 151 leave with no way of returning
apprehend 151 arrest
electrocution 152 death by means of electric shock
detection 152 being found out or seen
skirt 152 move along an edge
tree line 152 edge of a wooded area or jungle, w/ trees on one side and bare land, beach, etc. on the other
shinny 152 climb by gripping alternately with arms and legs to pull oneself up
jolt 153 a sudden, heavy blow
tailbone 153 bone at the end of the spinal column; the coccyx
alibi 153 defense against an accusation of committing a crime by proving one was elsewhere
impassive 154 showing no feelings
unanticipated 154 not expected
neutral 154 showing no feelings
electrocuted 155 shocked, injured, or killed by electric shock
excruciating 155 extremely painful
emphatically 155 forcefully
slag heap 155 a pile of waste from coal mining
contrite 156 apologetic; sorry

knocked up 156 pregnant (slang)
indignation 157 anger at an injustice or unfairness
lapse 157 omission; failure
wince 158 slight, involuntary grimace (narrowing one's eyes) or shrinking from sudden physical or emotional pain
dispatched 158 sent
hassock 158 padded footstool
chamomile 158 herbal remedy for anxiety or trouble sleeping
inhibited 159 able to control behavior according to social expectations
tendrils 159 plant's thin, twisting structures to help it climb and grasp supports (figurative here & p. 296; literal on p. 300)
irrefutable 160 impossible to disprove
herbalist 162 person who specializes in the use of medicinal herbs
unnerve 162 upset; make nervous
propaganda 162 systematic delivery of persuasive information that supports a particular point of view
odious 162 inspiring hatred or revulsion; highly offensive
incorporated 163 combined w/

Journal and Discussion Questions

1. Explain the stages of Katniss's response to her discovery that the fence is electrified.
2. What are the factors that contribute to Katniss's decision to jump from a 25-foot high branch?
3. List all the steps Katniss takes to conceal how she spent the day.
4. What is the first sign that each person at Katniss's home (besides the Peacekeepers) gives that shows that he or she understands what Katniss is trying to do and is working to help her?
5. What do you think is the word that Peeta whispered and Katniss didn't quite catch? Explain the reasons behind your suggestion.
6. Do you think Snow and Thread are acting together or separately? What evidence supports your answer?
7. In what context was the family book important in *The Hunger Games*? Explain the meaning you make from its repeated appearance.
8. Based on Katniss's descriptions (pp. 27, 95, 161), compare and contrast Gale's and Peeta's hands. What do you gather from the parallel?
9. Explain Katniss's reasoning about District 13 in this chapter.
10. Summarize the chapter from Mrs. Everdeen's point of view.

Summary

Upon recognizing that the fence is on, Katniss immediately backs up into the trees, covering her mouth to conceal the white puffs of her breath, and wondering whether electrifying the fence is a general security precaution or aimed specifically at catching her outside the district in order to punish her. She suspects the latter, which makes it her job to get back inside as quickly as possible without being seen and pretend she never left. She wonders if a spy saw Gale kiss her or if there are surveillance cameras.

She rules out burrowing under the fence, and the alternative is finding a tree with a branch at least 20-feet high and extending well over the fence. Spotting a maple that meets these criteria, she is forced to climb a neighboring tree and leap across because the maple trunk has too large a diameter for her to climb. She jumps from the branch, hitting the ground with a jolt and falling back on her rear end, injuring her left heel and her tailbone. Though in pain, she can walk. So she heads to town to forge an alibi, purchasing bandages and sweets for Prim and planning a lie for her mother.

But when she arrives, she finds two Peacekeepers at the door of her kitchen, and from their surprise, understands that they knew she was in the woods and expected her to be trapped. They announce they have a message for her from Head Peacekeeper Thread and ask where she's been. She responds that it would be easier to say where she hasn't been, as she determinedly walks without limping to the table and sees that Haymitch and Peeta are there, besides her mother and Prim. She starts an argument with Prim over what she claims were inaccurate directions to the Goat Man, and Prim, Peeta, and Haymitch all offer support to her story, convincing the male Peacekeeper. But the woman Peacekeeper demands to see what's in Katniss's bag, so she dumps out the bandages and candy. The message turns out the be that the fence is now electrified 24 hours a day, and she's to tell her "cousin." She promises to do so, adding that they'll all sleep more peacefully with this additional security.

The Peacekeepers leave, and Peeta helps Katniss to a rocker, and—knowing the house is bugged—she tells them she slipped on the ice. Her mother checks her feet and tailbone and treats her while Katniss eats. Prim makes Katniss promise to wait until Prim gets home from school before trying on wedding gowns, and Peeta carries her up to bed, and sits with her while the sleep syrup her mother gave her takes effect. Her last words are, "stay with me," and he answers with a single word she doesn't catch. Mrs. Everdeen orders a week of bed rest, giving Katniss plenty of time to think about Bonnie and Twill, the wedding dresses, and whether or not Thread and President Snow are in league, or if Thread is acting on his own. When no Peacekeepers show up to arrest her, she reasons that Thread must be trying to catch her red-handed.

Peeta lets her know that they're securing the base of the fence to the ground and visits every day to deliver cheese buns and help her with the family book. Like her father before her, Katniss is now adding her knowledge to the book, with Peeta doing the illustrations, which Peeta realizes is the first time they've ever done anything normal together. When Peeta carries Katniss downstairs each afternoon, she turns on the television, searching for the evidence that would show that the Capitol was hiding something about District 13, and in fact, she does see that a reporter of a current story has been incorporated into the same old footage with the mockingjay, leading to the question, if what they're showing is not what's in District 13, what *is* there?

Chapter 11, cont.

Catching Fire: A Teaching Guide 51

Chapter 12

The Prep Team Arrives; The Quarter Quell Card

Vocabulary

deemed 164 judged
histrionics 164 exaggerated, highly emotional displays of behavior
headpiece 166 any kind head covering
ivory 166 off-white color between yellowish white and grayish yellow
greenery 166 MM plant greens used for decoration
sheath 166 MM close-fitting dress w/ a narrow, tapered skirt
interference w/ 167 getting in the way of

shorthand 168 abbreviated language
cower 168 hide in a state of terror
nuclear weapons 168 weapons powered by energy released from an atom's nucleus
sarcasm 168 mockery; irony
nuptials 170 wedding ceremony
culminating 170 reaching a climax
invested in 170 devoted to; committed to
sweetshop 172 candy store
baffled 173 confused; at a loss

Journal and Discussion Questions

1. What does the prep team indirectly reveal about Panem's economic system?
2. Explain Katniss's "dough" simile.
3. Why would people feel less vulnerable when winter ends?
4. Evaluate Haymitch's prediction about the Capitol's choice of retaliations.
5. Haymitch provides further arguments for why District 12 isn't ready to revolt. What makes this important to Katniss in a personal way?
6. What has led to the enormous investment of Capitol residents in the choice of wedding dress for a girl in District 12?
7. Compare and contrast the three Quarter Quell cards and the "usual" reaping procedure. What gives each one its particular horror?
8. Summarize the chapter from Prim's point of view.

Summary

Once Katniss sees the footage that verifies that the Capitol may be covering up something about District 13, she has a harder time staying in bed to recuperate. Gradually, she rehabs her foot. Just when she's decided she's well enough to go to town, her prep team arrives, a bit early for Haymitch's pushed back date to accommodate the healing of Katniss's face. Usually Katniss ignores her prep team's "news," but the comment that they can't get shrimp, supposedly because of the bad weather in District 4, gets her attention. It turns out, they've been having trouble getting electronics (District 3) and fabric (District 8), as well as seafood, and Katniss surmises a growing rebellion.

Cinna adjusts her makeup and the photo shoot commences and moves from dress to dress to dress, with Katniss hoping to have a chance to talk to Cinna. But as soon as they're done, Effie ushers all district personnel out the door. Katniss realizes that her mother and Prim are inordinately happy about the photo shoot because they believe it means that Katniss is safe.

Waking early with nightmares, Katniss feels in need of a confidant, and—having missed Peeta—goes by Haymitch's house. He suggests a walk to town. She relays the information about Bonnie and Twill and the shortages in the Capitol. Haymitch still thinks District 12 is not ready for rebellion and is unconvinced about District 13. He predicts that if the uprisings get worse, the Capitol won't have reservations about destroying another district, as they did 13. Prim comes home from school expecting that Katniss's photo shoot will be televised this very evening, since her teachers have said there is mandatory programming. Katniss doubts they could be ready that fast, and reflects that she hasn't been able to prepare Gale for seeing her in a wedding dress. Prim is right, and Katniss learns that Cinna actually designed two dozen gowns, which Capitol residents had already voted on, narrowing the choice to the six dresses that are featured, modeled by Katniss, in a show with Caesar Flickerman and Cinna present, and the footage of Katniss fit in. As Katniss is about to turn the television off, Caesar mentions a following big event, and Mrs. Everdeen correctly suggests that it may be the "reading of the card." President Snow appears with a young boy carrying a wooden box. Snow recalls the previous Quells and their cards, and when he recalls the 50th anniversary quell, Mrs. Everdeen says that her friend Maysilee Donner went that year, and that's the first Prim and Katniss have ever heard of her. Snow chooses the card marked 75 from the box and reads that the tributes for the 75th Quarter Quell will come from existing victors, causing immediate reactions from Mrs. Everdeen and Prim. It takes Katniss a moment before she realizes that this means she's heading back into the arena.

Strategy 15

Interpreting Intentional Contradictions

In mysteries, thrillers, and tales of political intrigue, authors purposely present conflicting information. In mysteries, this puts the reader in a similar position to the detective and is a fundamental aspect of the genre. In all these genres, planned contradictions are realistic (the devious, and the power hungry often lie, cheat, and mislead) and create suspense. Even books in other genres may have intentional contradictions.

Contradictions can arise from several different causes:

- A character (including the narrator) telling a lie or giving a false impression through actions or words inherently creates a contradiction.
- A character's misinterpretation is another way apparent contradictions can arise.
- Characters reasoning from insufficient information can lead to apparent contradictions.
- A change or new development can lead to an actual or apparent contradiction or create discontinuity from the characters' point of view.

Collins uses all these types of contradiction in her trilogy.

- **Lie or Purposeful False Impression.** Katniss works to create the impression that she is in love with Peeta, although she is not. At Haymitch's instruction, Katniss and Peeta each conceal their outstanding skill from the other tributes.
- **Misinterpretation.** Katniss draws mistaken conclusions about Peeta from misinterpreting his choices and motives. A member of the Career Pack makes a mistake in assuming the tribute he knifed is dead.
- **Insufficient Evidence.** Katniss and Peeta draw incorrect conclusions about Haymitch from insufficient evidence: he is more than just a drunkard. Haymitch's strategy for Katniss and Peeta in the arena is his best guess, but had Katniss heeded it and not picked up the backpack and sheet of plastic, she probably would have died.
- **Change.** The changes in the Hunger Games rules create contradictions for Katniss and Peeta in deciding which strategies to pursue.

The results for the reader's experience are various, depending on the particular contradiction. Some contradictions move the plot forward; some provide suspense; some engage the reader in reflecting on the text. So if you find a contradiction as you read, you should consider if it is intentional, caused by one of the four listed causes and aimed at one of these results. (Contradictions can also occur due to a mistake by the writer; we'll discuss that possibility in Strategy 18: Considering Possible Continuity Issues.)

1. Examine the contradictory evidence about District 13. As far as you can tell, which of the four causes—Lie or False Impression; Misinterpretation; Insufficient Evidence; and/or Change—is/are responsible for the contradiction. Explain.
2. Examine the contradictory evidence about the potential for Katniss to help lead an uprising. As far as you can tell, which of the four causes—Lie or False Impression; Misinterpretation; Insufficient Evidence; and/or Change—is/are responsible for the contradictions. Explain.

Directions:
First, read the information. Then, answer the question or questions.

Strategy 16

Considering Possible Consistency Issues

You may be familiar with the term **continuity** from movie reviews. Typically, this term comes up when someone's hairstyle or shirt color changes in mid-scene with no explanation, although errors can also be more important. This kind of mistake can mar a movie's consistency more or less, depending on how important and obvious the mistake is.

Books can also have continuity errors, but they are part of a larger category of **consistency issues** and are often more subtle because they require reasoning, rather than visual observation, to uncover. We can categorize consistency issues into three main areas:

- **Internal Consistency.** This includes all the items that are considered continuity issues in movies: mistakes in keeping the world of the story consistent.
- **External Consistency.** This includes all items that violate "real life." How and when one looks for external consistency is guided by which elements of the story are presented as being like the real world.
- **Genre Consistency.** This includes stories straying from their declared genre without the author intentionally making the choice (and in some cases, explicitly without explicitly notifying readers).

While it's easy to scrub back and forth in a video and determine that a character's part changed sides, it's often more difficult to determine that the writer of a novel made a mistake in the plot line or has described an event that is well nigh impossible (but is intended to seem factually accurate). For this reason, it's important to consider carefully whether there might be an alternative explanation before deciding the writer has made a mistake.

Here's an example. In Chapter 1 (p. 10) of *Catching Fire*, Katniss is in the Hob. Here she purchases a list of items, including buns. Now, elsewhere she is described as living next door to Peeta who keeps all of them "in fresh baked goods" (p. 15). So this might seem like a mistake—a continuity error. But continuing reading through the first paragraph on page 16, we learn that there is distance and tension between Katniss and Peeta. In light of this, Katniss purchasing a bun could be symbolic of this disconnect, rather than an error. In fact, not eating Peeta's bread seems like a really good symbol of Katniss rejecting the love story she was forced into in the arena in order to stay alive. Verdict: intentional and meaningful; not an inconsistency.

An example of a true continuity error might be Katniss's leap from the maple tree, hike to town, shopping tour of the square, and walk home, given the extent of her injuries that require a lengthy period of recovery. Granted, this is a young woman who's experienced serious pain in life-threatening situations and had to bite the bullet and do what needed to be done. But it's questionable whether it would truly be possible.

1. In Chapter 12, Katniss goes to turn the television off. If she had, her family would have missed the announcement of the Quarter Quell and the reading of the card. Given information in the first two books of the trilogy, this seems like a continuity error. Explain the contradictions in this scene, citing evidence from other places in the trilogy. Tell why you think Collins wrote this scene in this way.

Directions: First, read the information. Then, answer the question or questions.

Chapter 13

Katniss and Haymitch Make a Deal; Training; Reaping

Chapter 13
Page 174

Vocabulary

shafts 174 rays
hysteria 174 uncontrolled emotional outburst
multitude 174 large number
sheeting 175 drop cloth
embodiment 175 living representation
tuckered out 176 worn out (rural dialect)
obligated 177 required
brusquely 178 shortly; curtly
sloshing 179 splashing
parched 180 dry
bile 180 bitter fluid from the liver used in digestion of fats: it makes up the substance of vomit when no food is left in the system
erratic 181 unplanned and irregular
self-righteous 183 sure of being in the right
dregs 183 particles that settle at the bottom of bottles of liquor
bonding 184 becoming friends with
copious 184 a large amount of
sultry 185 hot and humid
procedure 185 sequence of steps required in a given situation
pureed 189 blended until smooth
durable 190 sturdy; long-lasting
wafer 190 thin, crisp cracker
dabbing at 190 patting
linen 190 cloth made from the fibers of the flax plant

Journal and Discussion Questions

1. How is Katniss's use of the drop cloth at the house she runs to reminiscent of the Hunger Games? What is the effect of this parallel?
2. In what way(s) is Peeta "superior" to Katniss and Haymitch?
3. Why does Gale suggest running away again at this point? What conclusions do you draw?
4. On p. 30 Katniss crushes a cookie and then explains the symbolism of her action. On p. 179, Katniss drops the liquor bottle and then explains the symbolism of her action. What do you make of the way Collins chose to approach these situations?
5. It could be said that in a number of ways that she has not acknowledged, Katniss's comment (p. 31) about always having to protect her mother is untrue, either because her mother proves to have the strength to bear what comes or because her mother is protecting Katniss. Identify the evidence up to and including this chapter that supports this claim.
6. How is District 12's reaping for the Quarter Quell different than its reaping for the 74th Hunger Games?
7. How do changes in this chapter create discontinuity for Katniss?
8. Summarize the chapter by explaining the ways in which Gale's view of the events of this chapter and Peeta's view of the events are similar and differ.

Summary

Katniss's first instinct upon learning that she will be a tribute in the Quarter Quell is to run to the woods, and she stops only when she hears the hum of the fence. She heads back to the Victor's Village and ends up in the cellar of one of the empty houses. Overcome with hysteria, she stuffs her shirt in her mouth and screams until she's almost lost her voice. She never imagined a return to the arena as a possibility, partly because victors have always been exempt from further reaping, partly because she has been focusing on either her forced future with Peeta or her dangerous future as a rebel. As she pulls some sheeting over herself for warmth, she hears someone calling her, but ignores the call, choosing to focus just on herself for the moment.

Katniss reflects that it seems unlikely that 75 years ago, this seemingly perfect response to the Capitol's current problems of Katniss's widespread influence and the spreading unrest would have been put in place. The death of the victors, who embody hope for the districts, would be a clear demonstration that there is no hope. Glad that she doesn't know the other victors—who return to the Capitol each year as mentors or guests and whom she thinks are mutual friends—Katniss suddenly realizes that the people she has to worry about having to kill are Peeta and Haymitch and immediately thinks that she can't kill either of them. Perhaps they have already come to an arrangement she thinks, sure that Peeta will insist that even if Haymitch is chosen, Peeta be allowed to go into the arena to protect Katniss.

As she leaves the house, she discovers broken glass in the kitchen door, which

Chapter 13, cont.

explains to her why her hand is bleeding. Heading to Haymitch's house, she finds him drunk, and when he asks what she wants, after a little reflection, she asks for a drink. Haymitch tells her that Peeta argued that since last time Haymitch chose Katniss, he now owes Peeta anything Peeta wants, and what Peeta wants is to go in the arena with Katniss, who is mortified that while she was thinking only of herself, Peeta was thinking of how to save her. They agree that Peeta is the best person of the three of them and that Katniss doesn't deserve him. And Katniss figures out what she wants to ask Haymitch: that they try to save Peeta this time. Seeing his look of pain, she points out that—given the Capitol's hatred—she's as good as dead and that it's Peeta's turn to be saved. Haymitch agrees. She heads home with a bottle and is greeted at the door by Gale who tells her they should have run away and that it's not too late, but—looking at her mother and Prim—Katniss says it *is* too late, because she's sure if she runs now, they will die, plus she is committed to protecting Peeta.

She drops the bottle as she blacks out. She wakes up to vomit and shower and notices stitches in her hand. Back in bed, she hears footsteps and prepares to be calm and positive, but when their mother and Prim enter, she bursts into tears, and they comfort her. She goes back to sleep, waking in the early afternoon, when she gets up, dresses, and forgives herself for the one day of indulgence. She drinks a mug of broth and takes a mug to Haymitch. Peeta enters, announcing that he's emptied out all of Haymitch's liquor and there's no room on their team for drunkards. He's already asked Effie for tapes of all the living victors so they can learn about how the others fight, and he plans for the District 12 team to act like Careers in preparing for the arena. Soon, Katniss and Haymitch agree, and the group spends evenings watching Game recaps, mornings doing strengthening exercises, and afternoons working on combat skills. When Katniss wonders why they never met any of the other victors on the Victory Tour, Haymitch says President Snow wouldn't have wanted anyone to see them bonding with other victors. Katniss teaches the men to climb trees, and on Sundays, Gale teaches them about snares. Gale tells Katniss, as she walks him back to town one night, that he wishes Peeta were easier to hate. Katniss conjectures that in that case, Peeta would have died in the arena, and she'd have been the sole victor. Gale asks where that would leave the two of them, and Katniss equivocates, saying they'd be hunting, as they usually did on Sundays. Katniss reflects that Gale knows she chose him over Peeta when she didn't run, and that's as much as she can give. She doesn't want him to get emotional and do something drastic before the Quell, and since she doesn't plan on coming back, she doesn't want to give him hope. She plans some parting words for the farewell ceremony after the reaping, but she doesn't get the chance to speak them. Her name is drawn, then Haymitch's, and Peeta volunteers to replace him. But instead of having the opportunity to say goodbye to loved ones, Head Peacekeeper Thread takes them immediately to the train, and with no cameras or crowds of well-wishers, they set off to the Capitol.

Chapter 14

Other Victors; How Haymitch Won the Quell

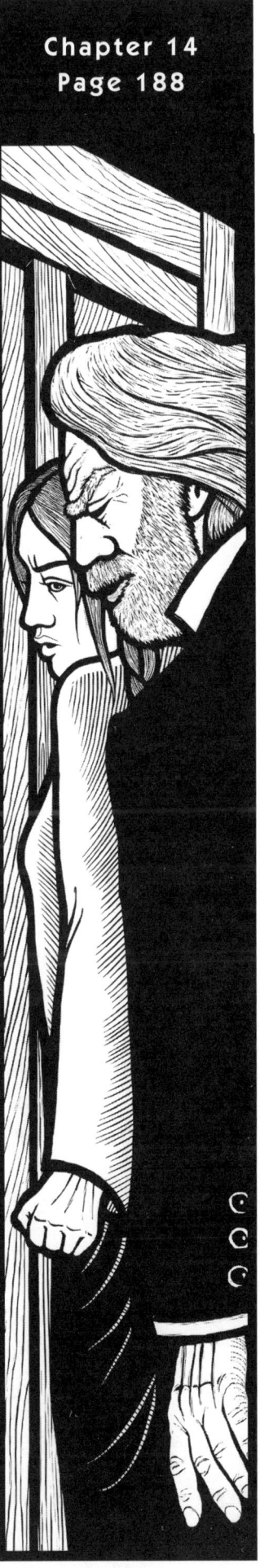

Chapter 14
Page 188

Vocabulary

studiously 191 in a thoughtful way
devoid of 191 not having
gooseflesh 192 nickname for bumps on skin caused by fear or cold temperatures
onerous 196 weighty; laborious
smash cut 196 sudden change of scene w/out transition
disengages 196 removes
snarky 197 snide; rude and sarcastic
knit 198 draw together in a frown
azure 198 bright, deep blue
aerial 198 from overhead
crystalline 198 pure and transparent
carnivorous 199 meat-eating
blowgun 199 narrow pipe for shooting darts with one's breath
darts MM 199 small, pointed missiles shot from a blowgun

picturesque 199 suitable for a picture
blowtorch 201 portable device that mixes oxygen w/ other gases to produce a flame
dislodges 201 knocks loose
abyss 201 a very deep chasm or gorge
lobs 201 throws w/ a high arc; tosses
vie 201 compete
inevitable 201 impossible to prevent or avoid
disarmed 201 deprived of any weapon
intestines 201 passage from the stomach to the anus
makes a beeline for 201 heads directly to; speedily follows the most direct path to
swig 202 gulp
sobriety 202 staying sober,

Journal and Discussion Questions

1. List Katniss's take-aways from watching the reaping recaps.
2. Explain the change in the dynamic between Katniss and Peeta in this chapter.
3. What do you think the announcer is expecting to occur in the Games that leads her to say it will be the best ever?
4. No Capitol attendants on the train or in the Training Center spoke in *The Hunger Games*, and some—if not all of them—were Avoxes. Explain the narrative function of having the attendant who brings the milk speak. In your opinion, was it worth the apparent inconsistency to achieve this? Explain why you think as you do.
5. Katniss uses the term *smash cut*. Explain the narrative purpose of its use. Then either defend her use of it or explain why you believe it's a continuity error.
6. Katniss says that the second Quarter Quell was never shown on television because it made the Capitol look bad. So why would the Capitol allow unedited copies to be handed out? Either defend the tape's availability or tell why you believe that its appearance represents a continuity error. Explain why you think Collins wrote the scene in this way.
7. What similarities between Katniss and Haymitch are revealed in this chapter?
8. How does material in this chapter explain something that surprised Katniss when she was in school?
9. Summarize the chapter from Haymitch's point of view.

Summary

Katniss continues looking out the window after she can no longer see District 12, reaffirming her commitment to never return. She thinks about how she'd worked out the words to leave her loved ones behind, and now that's been taken away by the Capitol, too. Peeta suggests writing letters, and while Katniss nods agreement, she knows she won't write, not being gifted with words. She realizes she must complete her mourning if she wants to accomplish her mission to save Peeta, so she endeavors to let her loved ones go.

At dinner, when Peeta compliments Effie's hair, she says it was done to match Katniss's pin, and speculates about getting items for Haymitch and Peeta as well. Katniss surmises that Effie doesn't know that the pin is a symbol used by the rebels, and that real rebels wouldn't put their secret symbol on something solid like jewelry, but on wafers that could be eaten for concealment, should the need arise. Peeta is enthusiastic, and Haymitch agrees, but because he is continuing to stay sober, he's miserable.

They gather to watch the reapings, which include 59 living victors of the 75 who have been chosen, with the Career districts—1, 2, and 4—having the largest pools. Haymitch is stoic, Effie sighs, Peeta stars the name in his notebooks, and Katniss tries to make a

Catching Fire: A Teaching Guide 57

Chapter 14, cont.

mental record, but doesn't do very well, noting the names of only Brutus from 2, Finnick from 4, Johanna from 7, Cecilia from 8, and Chaff—a friend of Haymitch's—from 11. The announcer comments that the star-crossed lovers can't get a break, but then voices her expectation of "the best Games ever." Haymitch and Effie leave, and Peeta suggests that Katniss get some sleep while he reviews his notes. Though she wants Peeta with her, she can't ask him because they've barely touched since Gale was whipped.

After the first nightmare, Katniss leaves her room and—ordering warm milk from an attendant—finds Peeta still in the TV room, watching the old tapes Effie had sent him. When she acknowledges nightmares, Peeta holds out his arms to her, and she walks into his embrace, and—having said goodbye to Gale and having no expectation of ever seeing him again—concludes that nothing she does can hurt him: he won't see a great deal, and what he does see, he'll think is acting. The attendant brings an extra cup and adds honey and spice – indicating to Peeta that people in the Capitol feel bad for the victors going back into the arena, an interpretation which Katniss dismisses. Peeta gives Katniss the pick of the next tape, and she selects the second Quarter Quell, even though she feels that it broaches Haymitch's privacy. They plan not to tell Haymitch they watched it.

As they watch, they see Maysilee Donner chosen and realize that she was both Mrs. Everdeen's friend and Madge's aunt, and, in retrospect, understand the pain of Madge's mother, Madge's bringing the medicine to Gale, and a different meaning for the mockingjay pin. Katniss hopes that Haymitch didn't kill Maysilee, and Peeta remarks that with so many tributes, the odds are against it. Because Haymitch won, they see his interview, in which his basic personality—snide, arrogant, and distant—is exhibited. The arena for the Quell is breathtakingly beautiful, which disorients and slows down many of the players, but not Haymitch, who immediately arms himself with weapons and a backpack at the Cornucopia and heads for the woods. Eighteen players die in the bloodbath and the quick deaths of many others reveals that just about all the beautiful natural objects are deadly. Ten well-provisioned Careers have teamed up and are out hunting in the area of a mountain. Haymitch fights carnivorous squirrels and stinging butterflies, but continues trekking away from the mountain. Maysilee resourcefully turns a blowgun she gets at the Cornucopia into a deadlier weapon by poisoning the darts. On the fourth day, the mountain turns out to be a volcano, taking out 12 more tributes, including five of the Careers. So that leaves 13 tributes, who are now all in the woods. Haymitch continues moving in one direction until he meets a maze of hedges, which forces him back towards the center of the woods, where he encounters three Careers. He kills two and is saved from the third by a dart from Maysilee, who proposes an alliance. Haymitch accepts, and their conversation reveals that Haymitch is seeking the edge of the arena, not sure what he'll find, but hoping for something useful. What they find is a cliff. Maysilee doesn't want to stay near the edge, partly so it doesn't come down to the two of them, so they part with five tributes left. Haymitch accidentally discovers the electrical field that throws back anything that falls or is thrown at it. Then Maysilee's screams send Haymitch running to her aid, despite the broken alliance. When he reaches her, she's dying from a bird attack, and all he can do is hold her hand as she dies. Two more tributes die, leaving Haymitch and a District 1 girl. Both have received deadly wounds when Haymitch is disarmed and makes for the cliff. He reaches it and falls to the ground just as she throws an ax, which flies over his head and into the abyss. The girl is thinking she's won when it flies back and hits her in the head.

Peeta identifies the similarity between the force field at the edge of the arena and the one on the roof of the Training Center. Katniss points out that it wasn't meant to be a weapon, so Haymitch's win was similar to theirs, but Haymitch, who has quietly joined them with a bottle of wine, says it's not quite the same. Nevertheless, Katniss feels a newfound confidence knowing who her teammates are.

Writer's Forum 5

Writing a Letter of Farewell

A **farewell letter** can range from very informal to extremely formal. It might be as simple as "It's been good being your neighbor—I hope we meet again!" followed by initials. In general, the more significant the relationship, the longer, more serious, and more intimate such a letter will be.

Personal farewell letters are generally written by hand, partly because they're often informal, and partly because they're personal. Word processing is used for more formal thanks via snail mail or email, or for expressing thanks within the context of a business relationship. When it does not require the formality of a business letter, a farewell letter may take the form of a personal letter.

Personal letters differ from business letters in the following ways:
- They include only the date, not the return address in the **heading**.
- They do not include an **inside address**.
- The **salutation** ends with a comma, rather than a colon.
- Each paragraph of the **body** is indented, not put in block form.
- The **closing** is friendly and personal and followed by a comma.
- The **signature** may be a nickname or pet name.
- They are usually handwritten rather than typed.

_____	Date
____,	Salutation followed by comma
_____	Body with indented paragraphs
____,	Closing followed by comma
	Handwritten signature

Farewell letters often acknowledge gratitude and express thanks, using words such as:
- thank you (very much)
- appreciate
- gratitude
- your thoughtfulness
- pleased
- your kindness

1. Suppose that Peeta, following up on his own idea, sends a letter to his father. Considering Peeta and what you know of his relationship with his father, his current situation, and his plans, write a letter that he might have sent. Remember to stay in character.

Directions: First, read the information. Then, answer the question or questions.

**Chapter 15
Page 262**

Chapter 15

Meeting Victors and Chariot Ride; the New Avox

Vocabulary

console 204 comfort
headlamps 205 lights worn on headbands or the fronts of helmets when underground
deceptively 206 falsely
embers 206 smoldering pieces of coal
bejeweled 207 decorated in jewels
trident 209 three-pronged spear
extension 209 addition
entangle 209 trip up
drooling over 209 looking at w/ desire
retains 209 keeps
extravagant 209 unreasonably expensive

sensuous 209 appealing to the senses
groin 209 area where the thighs join the torso
salivating 210 drooling
devastating 210 deeply hurtful
saunters 210 walks in a leisurely way
seductive 211 intending to entice
amputate 214 remove; cut off
camaraderie 214 fellowship
headdress 214 covering for the head
stitch of clothing 215 any clothes

Journal and Discussion Questions

1. Compare and contrast how Peeta and Katniss become aware of the changing mood of Capitol citizens.
2. Explain how the Quarter Quell card has made the Capitol viewers of the games more like the District viewers.
3. Compare Katniss's assessment of her costume for the chariot ride in *Catching Fire* to her parallel comment in *The Hunger Games*. What conclusions can you draw?
4. Why do you think the District 12 team does not appear at the chariot send-off?
5. Katniss uses the phrase "while the life bled out of Gale." Analyze the phrase for its accuracy and tone.
6. Predict the effects Darius's presence as an Avox will have on Katniss.
7. Summarize the chapter from Peeta's point of view.

Summary

Katniss expects her intake prep to be the same as usual, so she is surprised to find her team distraught, and begins to give more thought to the effects of the Quell on the Capitol citizens. She's so irritable that she threatens to kill Cinna if he cries, and he explains that he channels his feelings into his work so he won't hurt anyone but himself. In contrast to last year, her makeup is dramatic, her outfit plain black, and she wears a victor's crown of black, but when Cinna presses a button, she becomes a glowing ember, making her look like a deadly force. He instructs her not to wave or smile, but to be indifferent to the crowd.

As Katniss waits for the chariots, she finds that this year's tributes and their mentors are talking in small groups. Knowing none of them, Katniss just hangs out with her horse until Finnick Odair of District 4, comes over, and eyes her seductively. He is known to have had numerous romances since he turned 16 (he won the games when he was 14) and confesses that he no longer deals in money, but is paid for his company in secrets. Peeta arrives just after Finnick leaves, and Katniss tells him of the strange meeting. With Portia, Cinna, and Haymitch absent, they decide to switch on their outfits, but are unsure whether they're "supposed to" hold hands—however they do. Katniss can see on the large screens that they seem dark, powerful, and unforgiving.

When they arrive back at the Training Center, Portia and Cinna are there, and Haymitch brings over the tributes from District 11, his friend Chaff—who has a stump without a prosthetic—and Seeder, a woman of about 60, who tells Katniss that Rue's and Thresh's families are alive. Chaff greets Katniss with a kiss on the mouth, which discomfits her and makes him and Haymitch laugh, and the Capitol attendants usher them to the elevators, seemingly desirous of limiting the interchanges between districts. They end up with Johanna Mason from District 7 who—disgusted with her costume— undresses piece by piece as they walk, entering the elevator with only her slippers on. Peeta interprets for Katniss that Johanna, Chaff, and Finnick are teasing her because she's prudish, but he's clearly amused, and this irritates Katniss. Haymitch and Effie get off the other elevator as they arrive. Katniss sees Haymitch's expression change as he looks past the tributes, and Effie mentions a "matched set." Turning to see what is going on, Katniss sees the redheaded Avox girl has been joined by Darius.

60 *Catching Fire: A Teaching Guide*

Chapter 16

Making Allies/Friends; Time with the Gamemakers

Chapter 16
Page 218

Vocabulary

rendered 218 made
power pack 219 portable source of power
clench 219 tight grip
clucking 219 making disapproving sounds
wedge 219 **MM** squeeze
wasn't Hob 220 idiom for belonging to the community who bought and sold at the District 12 black market
grotesque 220 ludicrous; bizarre; distorted
depicting 220 representing
put a positive spin on 221 interpret in a favorable way
dissection 221 act of cutting tissue apart
meandering 222 wandering
bangle 222 a rigid bracelet
shackle 222 metal fastening to hold a prisoner's ankles or wrists
exceptional 223 unusually good
fang 225 long, pointed tooth, like an animal's canine tooth
spiel 225 prepared speech
unfazed 225 not perturbed or upset
ashen 226 very pale
ribald 226 engaging in lewd humor
glitter 227 little bits of shiny, decorative material that reflects light

allude 227 make an indirect reference to
goblet 228 handleless drinking glass w/ a stem and base
chink in the armor 229 small, but potentially fatal, weakness
retort 230 answer sharply
sociable 231 friendly
hammocks 231 lengths of woven netting suspended to make resting places
garbled 232 confused
stroke 232 reduction or stoppage of blood supply to part of the brain, resulting in brain damage
wishbone 232 Y-shaped bone found in most fowl
airborne 232 into flight
exhibition 233 performance
invincible 234 unable to be defeated
creased 235 wrinkled
tidbits 235 choice bits of food
singling himself out 235 making himself stand out from the group
smug 236 self-satisfied and unconcerned about anything/anyone else
veneer 236 façade
dangles 236 hangs loosely

Journal and Discussion Questions

1. If Katniss is correct that President Snow personally planned for Darius to attend her at the Training Center, what does that suggest about the appearance of the redheaded girl Avox in *The Hunger Games* (and again in *Catching Fire*)? What conclusions can you draw?

2. Given the Capitol attendants' unease with the victor's camaraderie at the chariot ride, why isn't there more supervision and separation of districts enforced during training?

3. Read this account of the punishment of Tantalus from a Greek myth: http://www.mythweb.com/encyc/entries/tantalus.html and explain how it relates to this chapter.

4. Why do you think Plutarch won't meet Katniss's eye after having danced with her?

5. Explain why choosing allies is fraught for Katniss.

6. Speculate about:

    a. Peeta's demonstration—what did he do?

    b. the Gamemakers' response to Katniss's demonstration—how will they react?

7. Summarize the chapter by making a list of all the inter-district interactions mentioned.

Summary

As Katniss recognizes Darius, Haymitch grasps her wrist to keep her from acting impetuously, but she is aware that showing recognition would get him punished, so they just stare at each other. Katniss realizes that President Snow has placed Darius there to destabilize her. She sits in her room alone until dinner, then purposely knocks a dish of peas to the floor, and as Darius bends to clean them up, she does, too, and they clench hands until Effie chastises Katniss because cleaning up is a servant's job. When the team goes to watch the opening ceremonies recap, Katniss sits between Haymitch and Cinna—avoiding Peeta, both because her relationship with Darius was connected to the Hob and Gale and because she's still mad at him for laughing at her. Katniss thanks

Chapter 16, cont.

the stylists and heads to bed, ignoring a gentle knock on her door.

After nightmares involving tongues, she delays going to breakfast because she's not looking forward to discussing training strategies, even when Haymitch pounds on her door. When she finally joins them, she finds Haymitch wearing a gold "team 12" bangle and in a foul mood. He accosts her for being late, and though she means her apology to sound snarky, her voice catches at the end and Haymitch relents. He gives them two instructions: to continue to show that they're in love and to make friends. Katniss refuses immediately, but Haymitch points out that they're going to need more allies because they're at a disadvantage with all the other victors having known each other for years, making District 12 the first targets for everyone. Katniss takes this to mean they're doomed, since they can do nothing to influence long-standing friendships, but Haymitch points out that they're desirable allies, due to their ability to fight and popularity with the audience. Katniss wonders if he wants them to join up with the Careers, and he says they can form their own pack if they want, and suggests Chaff and Seeder, while mentioning that they shouldn't ignore Finnick, and should find people who will be of use to them.

Although Effie comes to escort them, Haymitch forbids it—he doesn't want them looking like they need a babysitter. Katniss suggests they split up to cover more ground, but then goes to the knot-tying station, which has no other tributes until Finnick comes and completes a knot for her. He then makes a noose and pretends to hang himself. Katniss heads to another empty station to work on starting fires without matches, and is just having some success when she is joined by the tributes from District 3. In order to be able to tell Haymitch that she tried, she stays and gets to know a little about Wiress, who truncates her sentences, and fidgety Beetee, both inventors. They carry on a conversation filled with hints and innuendos about the conditions in their districts, and move to the shelter station together, but Wiress pauses, pointing to the Gamemakers, and Katniss is able to see a bit of vibrating air, which Beetee identifies as a chink in the force field between tributes and Gamemakers, the reason for which Katniss explains. Before Katniss can ask more, it's lunchtime. Peeta's companions create one giant table forcing everyone to eat together. Meeting in the lunch line, Peeta reports that Wiress and Beetee are a joke to the other tributes, creating friction with Katniss, although he is just reporting information. Peeta asks why she's so angry and apologizes again, telling her they can be a team of two, but she says maybe Haymitch is right about alliances. Peeta is leaning towards Chaff and Seeder, but Katniss isn't okay with Chaff yet, so Peeta invites her to eat with Chaff, and her impression of him improves.

After lunch, Katniss tries to be friendly, doing an edible-insect station with District 8, hammocks with District 1, and fishhooks with Mags, Finnick's partner from District 4, who is old and seems to have had a stroke, and who Katniss wants on her team, which she's sure will not impress Haymitch. For escape, she goes to the archery station, where—the stationary targets providing no challenge—the trainer begins launching clay shooting pigeons, increasing the number of birds more and more as she hits every one. When she hits five in one round, she turns around to find she has an audience of most of the victors, with the result that when they arrive at dinner, half the victors have requested Katniss as an ally, puzzling Haymitch, who knows it wasn't for her personality, until Peeta explains that they saw her shoot, for real. Haymitch questions that she was good enough that Brutus would want to team up with her, but Katniss makes it clear that she doesn't want Brutus as an ally anyway, so Haymitch says he'll tell everyone she's still making up her mind. The upshot is, she no longer feels like an outsider. To give everyone a chance, she spends time with almost all the tributes, including an exchange of an hour of trident lessons for an hour of archery lessons with Finnick. But the better she gets to know them, the more awful the prospect of killing them to save Peeta becomes.

On the final day, when the sessions with the Gamemakers loom, the tributes joke about what they may do, with Mags, whom Katniss can understand better now, suggesting she'll take a nap. When they are the last two left, neither Peeta nor Katniss has decided what to do. Katniss abruptly asks how they're going to kill their fellow tributes, and Peeta has no answer. Katniss recalls her alliance with Rue, and Peeta says that Rue's death was the most despicable. Peeta goes in, and Katniss has to wait 40 minutes, though the sessions are only 15. When she is called, she finds a mat in the middle of the floor, covering something, and hopes that Peeta didn't make himself a target by what he did. But the Gamemakers are clearly upset, and Katniss wants to build on that and make them realize that they are vulnerable, too. Plutarch Heavensbee seems to be intentionally avoiding meeting her eye, and she recalls her dance with them. Then she gets an idea. She creates a noose, following Finnick's example, puts it around the neck of a target dummy, and finger paints the name Seneca Crane on its body, blocking their view of the words until she's done.

Strategy 17

Identifying Tropes— Chekhov's Gun

A literary **trope** is a device that has been widely used—enough so that many readers will recognize it. It may be a recurrent character type, plot development, setting, narrative device, or other literary technique (although these tropes may also be used in television shows, movies, and comics). Many tropes have been named in order to more easily identify and discuss their use. Tropes will be discussed in greater detail in the teaching guide for *Mockingjay*. The trope we're going to focus on here is called **Chekhov's Gun**.

Anton Chekhov (1860–1904), a Russian short story writer and playwright, is responsible for identifying and giving his name to this trope. In a letter to a colleague, Lazarev-Gruzinsky, in 1889, Chekhov wrote:

> "One should not put a loaded rifle onto the stage if no one is thinking of firing it. If in the first act you have hung a pistol on the wall, then in the following one, it should be fired, otherwise, don't put it there."

To look at it in a positive way: a seemingly unimportant object is introduced early on so that later it may take on a greater significance. Without this innocuous introduction, the appearance of an item or detail just when it becomes needed, can seem like such a long shot that it interrupts the reader's suspension of disbelief.

One example of an instance of Chekhov's Gun in the trilogy is the developing importance of the mockingjay pin—seemingly just a piece of jewelry when it was introduced—and the mockingjay itself. It is referred back to numerous times and developed into a symbol, acquiring a meaning beyond its literal depiction of a songbird, leading to the expectation that it will be used meaningfully.

1. Identify other instances of Chekhov's Gun in the portion of the trilogy you've read so far. Make a list, noting when each item is introduced and when it is used again. Continue to add to your list as you read.

Directions: First, read the information. Then, answer the question or questions.

Chapter 17

The Tributes Take Charge of the Interviews

Vocabulary

transgression 239 violation
brashness 239 rash behavior
impulsive 239 acting on sudden desires/ urges rather than well-thought-out plans
ruffled 239 upset; flustered
misty 240 sentimental; near tears
measured 240 carefully controlled
dovetails 244 interlocks; fits perfectly with
martyr 244 someone who dies for a cause;
obsessions with 247 irresistible fascination w/ and focus on
garment bag 247 hanging, often zippered, plastic sheath to protect clothing
decks ... out 248 dresses in special clothing and accessories
ravishing 248 lovely; extremely beautiful
bodice 248 the part of a dress from shoulder to waist

winging it 249 making it up on the spot, w/ out preparation
tuxedo 249 the usual men's fancy dress: trousers with a silk stripe down the side, jacket, bow tie, and cummerbund (wrap around the waist)
grooms 249 short for bridegrooms - men who are about to get or have recently been married
threshold 249 entrance; doorway
staring daggers 249 glaring at angrily or jealously
throwbacks 250 people who have more primitive character traits
legality 250 state of being in keeping with the law; state of being legal
bridal 251 wedding

Journal and Discussion Questions

1. How do you think the Gamemakers understood Katniss's presentation?
2. What do you think was "forbidden" about what Peeta did for the Gamemakers?
3. What do you make of Haymitch's response when Peeta tells him they don't want any allies?
4. Why is receiving the highest possible training score not a good thing?
5. Why does Katniss respond to Peeta by saying "To show them that I'm more than just a piece in their Games?"?
6. What does Katniss determine she can give the rebels while she's in the arena?
7. What does Katniss mean by suggesting she would be more valuable as a martyr?
8. In what way do Katniss's private and public agendas coincide?
9. What other events does Peeta's and Katniss's "day off" and how they spend it recall? What do you make of the parallels?
10. How do you explain the reactions of the other victors to Katniss's interview dress?
11. Summarize the chapter from Cinna's point of view.

Summary

The Gamemakers exhibit satisfying evidence of shock. Plutarch Heavensbee stares at Katniss while crushing a peach and dismisses her, and she tosses the rest of the berry juice over her shoulder onto the dummy as she leaves. Katniss feels an elation that she enjoys for the moment, expecting to pay for it later. She can't find Haymitch to tell him immediately, so she goes to shower. Only now does she consider whether her actions will serve Peeta, and deciding that even though they may not—for example, if the Gamemakers decide to punish her in the arena—she's still glad she did what she did.

As they gather for dinner, she notices stain on Peeta's hands. Haymitch's first question is about their private sessions. Neither wants to go first, but Peeta finally admits that he painted a picture of Rue, covered with flowers. In answer to Haymitch's question about what he meant to accomplish, Peeta says that he wanted to hold them accountable for killing her, even just for a moment, and both Effie and Haymitch find this disturbing, with Effie saying it's illegal. Katniss intervenes, saying that it's probably a bad time to mention that she hung Seneca Crane in effigy. In response, Effie leaves the table, and Peeta tells Haymitch they don't want allies. Haymitch responds that this decision frees him of responsibility for their killing his friends with their "stupidity." Effie rejoins them when they go to watch the training scores, and for the first time in history, there are two 12s awarded—to Peeta and Katniss—which Haymitch says is meant to force the other tributes to target them.

As they walk to their rooms, Peeta asks Katniss why she did what she did, and she quotes his words from the roof in *The Hunger Games*: "To show them that I'm more than just a piece in their Games?" which makes him laugh in recollection. They share the thought that President Snow has probably ordered the Gamemakers to make sure they die in the arena. But Katniss hopes that Snow will distinguish between them and let Peeta live, perhaps as a living warning. They agree that whatever happens, everyone will know that they went out fighting, and in that way, their actions will bring hope to the rebels, which to Katniss means that her private agenda and her public one coincide, for the moment.

Peeta says he wants to spend as much of the rest of his life with her as possible, so she pulls him into her room, and for the first time in a long time, neither of them has nightmares. The coaching sessions are canceled, ostensibly because they've been so recently coached for the Victory Tour, and they decide to spend the day on the roof, where they make up a game of catch that uses the force field and an apple, and relax. Katniss falls asleep with her head in Peeta's lap, but he wakes her for the sunset. They're not called for dinner, so they stay on the roof until bedtime, then retire to Katniss's room, where her prep team finds them in the morning, which makes Octavia start crying—so she has to leave, on Cinna's orders.

Prep is silent this time, and when Flavius starts crying, he too leaves, so Venia finishes, avoiding Katniss's gaze until the end when she tells Katniss for the whole team that it's been a privilege. Katniss asks Cinna what she's wearing for the interview, and he says that President Snow gave the order himself, revealing the wedding gown that garnered the most votes, and saying that the stylists' objections to this were ignored. Katniss finds it barbaric, and notes that the dress seems heavier, but Cinna claims he had to make alterations due to the lighting. He warns Katniss not to lift her arms above her head until she twirls, and adds that he's sure Caesar will suggest it, and she should if he doesn't, but only at the end of her interview. When they meet in the elevator, Katniss finds Peeta in a groom's garb, as worn in the Capitol. She recalls the simpler dress and the special District 12 ceremony of toasting. When they reach the backstage area, Katniss realizes that the other tributes are "staring daggers" at her dress, and the fact that some of them act sympathetic as well as angry confuses her. It isn't until the interviews start that Katniss can interpret this, as well as Johanna's comment to make Snow pay for it, as she sees how betrayed the victors, on the whole, feel. Aside from the Careers, the victors are united in doing their best to evoke the sympathy of the Capitol citizens and encouraging them to feel how unjust the re-reaping of the victors is. Katniss joins in, telling the audience how sorry she is that they won't get to see her wedding, and when she twirls to show them her wedding dress, the white features are burned away to reveal the black and white feathers of a mockingjay.

Chapter 17, cont.

Chapter 18

The Mockingjay Dress; Pregnancy; Attack on Cinna

Vocabulary

segue 254 transition
emanates 255 comes from
fuse 256 MM material along which a flame moves to explode a bomb, allowing the bomber time to escape
recoil 257 pull back
harried 258 harassed; agitated from dealing with multiple issues
second-guess 258 criticize after a decision has been made or an action has been taken

detract 258 take away from
empowered 258 filled w/ power; confident
fallout 258 side effects
appreciative 259 grateful
recklesss 262 done without attention to safety or consequences
metal-studded 262 covered with metal cleats or nails
undulating 263 moving like a wave

Journal and Discussion Questions

1. Given that most of the victors had decided to "build a bomb," why would they have "stared daggers" at Katniss's dress?
2. What is the significance of the audience's reactions?
3. Compare and contrast the pre-Game interviews in the two books.
4. What does Haymitch mean by his reminder to Katniss?
5. Make a list of all the ways Katniss has been targeted in this book.
6. Summarize this chapter by identifying Katniss's emotions at each key point.

Summary

Caesar tentatively identifies Katniss as a bird. She explains that she is the mockingjay from her token pin and sees that he understand what this will mean in the districts. He covers by switching focus to Cinna, which makes Katniss recall Cinna's words about channeling his feelings, and she fears for his safety. But by then, it is Peeta's turn. Skipping their usual banter, Caesar asks about the switch from wedding plans to preparing for the Quell. Peeta asks Caesar if he thinks the audience can keep a secret, which makes everyone uncomfortable, but Caesar says he's certain they can. Peeta confesses that he and Katniss are already married, not officially, but through their district ceremony of toasting, which they knew wouldn't be performed at their wedding in the Capitol, plus they didn't want to wait any longer. Caesar is sympathetic and says he's glad they've had some months of happiness, but Peeta says he wishes they had waited, which puzzles Caesar until Peeta explains that he, too, would have been glad of the few months if it weren't for the baby, thus igniting the "bomb" built by the efforts of the victors interviewed before him.

When the audience has digested this, Caesar can't get them back under control. When the anthem starts, Peeta takes Katniss's hand, and as she thinks of Rue's family, she offers her hand to Chaff, taking his stump. By the time the anthem ends, even the Careers who just want a good fight are part of an unbroken line of victors, all holding hands in an unprecedented sign of unity among the districts—the first since the rebellion. As soon as the camera crew realizes, the screens start to go black, but everyone's already seen. The lights go out and the Peacekeepers herd the victors to separate elevators by district. Peeta asks Katniss if he has to apologize for anything, and she says no. When they reach their floor, Haymitch tells them the recap of the interviews tomorrow has been canceled, and Peeta asks if the Capitol residents—who can be seen on the streets—will ask for the Games to be stopped. Haymitch says the Games will not be stopped and that he is the only one left: the others were all sent home. They ask Haymitch to thank Effie for them, and Haymitch gives them his usual advice to "stay alive," but adds to Katniss that in the arena, she should remember who the enemy is. Katniss persuades Peeta not to go to his room, and they hold each other all night, but aren't sure if they actually sleep.

Cinna and Portia come at dawn. They go to the roof to meet the hovercraft, and the tributes are injected with trackers. In the launch room, Cinna prepares Katniss, and they try to make inferences about the arena from the clothing. Then they hold hands until it's time for launch preparation, but when Katniss steps on the launch pad, the platform doesn't lift. Three Peacekeepers burst in and beat Cinna with gloves studded with metal, finally dragging his limp body from the room, while Katniss screams and bangs on the glass. The plate rises, and Katniss finds herself surrounded by water, and thinks that this environment is not a fitting place for a girl on fire.

Test: Chapters 10–18

Vocabulary

Look at each group of words. Tell why it is important in the story.

1. strawberry birthmark, quaver, malnourished
2. granary, armory, lockdown
3. footage, nuclear development, delusions
4. shinny, jolt, tailbone, alibi
5. slag heap, knocked up, indignation
6. headpiece, ivory, greenery, sheath
7. luscious, crystalline, azure, picturesque
8. mute, clench, clucking, wedge
9. metallic gold, bangle, shackle
10. chink, sociable, hammocks, wishbone
11. ravishing, bodice, staring daggers, bridal
12. harried, fallout, commotion

Essay Topics

1. Writers can signal to readers how carefully they should be reading. Take the case of Peeta complimenting Effie's new hairstyle on the train (p. 189). Understanding the compliment and the ensuing conversation requires knowing that Effie's hair is now "metallic gold"—a detail that appears in the previous chapter (p.186). Discuss whether consistently reading *Catching Fire* with this close attention is rewarded by increased understanding. Provide support for your stance.

2. Finnick says that if he and Katniss see something sweet, they'd better grab it while they can. Compare and contrast this to the sentiments expressed in the Robert Herrick poem "To the Virgins, to Make Much of Time" http://www.bartleby.com/101/248.htm

3. Considering the power the Quarter Quell card acknowledges that the victors have and the Peacekeepers' efforts to separate them after the interviews, either defend the fact that they are ever allowed to mingle and become friends at all or explain why you believe there is a continuity error. In either case, explain the narrative purpose.

4. A eulogy is a spoken or written tribute to someone, often—but not always—someone who has recently died. Though Cinna's fate is unknown, it is a fitting moment to assess his role. Write a tribute to Cinna in which you document his achievements, his importance to Katniss, and his larger impact, and include an anecdote that reveals a key trait.

5. Compare and contrast the wedding customs of the Capitol and District 12.

6. In retrospect, do you think Katniss's comment to Cinna that she is "winging it" in the interview this year is meant to be a pun? Explain both why you think as you do and the impact on the reader who does think it is a pun, even if you don't.

7. So far in *Catching Fire*, several unprecedented things have happened. List them and tell what you think the fact that they happened means.

8. Explain why you think Peeta's revelation of Katniss's pregnancy sends the Capitol citizen audience out of control. Use details from the text to support your stance.

Chapter 19

PART III: "THE ENEMY" Unexpected Alliance; Peeta Electrocuted

Vocabulary

plumage 267 feathers
emboldened 267 made bolder
white-hot 268 so hot that it glows white
radiating 268 extending in straight lines from a center; see MM on p. 124
wedge 268 **MM** shaped like a slice of pie
converging 269 coming together
impales 270 pierces; skewers
awl 271 pointed hand tool for making holes
submerges 272 goes underwater
altercation 272 fight; quarrel
abdomen 272 belly

cover me 272 protect me from attack
warding off 272 preventing an attack
propels 273 provides power for; pushes
flotation 274 make floating possible
obsolete 275 old-fashioned; barely used
evaporate 275 turn from liquid into vapor
specimen 275 example
massacre 276 kill without holding back
premature 278 in advance of what is expected, suitable, or desirable
intensifies 278 makes stronger
warped 278 twisted

Journal and Discussion Questions

1. Make a 2D or 3D depiction of the arena, adding as you continue reading.
2. What surprises Katniss and what shocks her in this chapter?
3. Explain what you suspect is Finnick's motivation and tell why you think so.
4. What do you think Peeta is thinking as he steps between Katniss and Finnick.
5. Identify the major confrontation(s) in Act 2 of *Catching Fire*. How do they follow from the first plot point? What is the second plot point/reversal?
6. Use the Choice Analysis Tool to analyze the first deaths in the Quarter Quell.

Summary

Claudius Templesmith announces the beginning of the 75th Hunger Games, and Katniss's ability to use the minute of waiting time to plan is impaired by her memories of Cinna's beating, though she knows it was meant to disconcert her. She decides she owes it to Cinna and the rebels who he may have inspired to focus. She discerns a tropical environment and the Cornucopia on a circular island with 12 spokes, and two tributes on metal plates between each pair of spokes. She smells and tastes the water, and judges it to be saltwater. When the gong sounds, Katniss dives to her left, notices that she seems buoyant, and makes for the nearest spoke of sandy land, which she runs down toward the Cornucopia, where all the supplies are piled, and immediately grabs a golden bow. Hearing someone, she arms her bow as she turns to face Finnick, armed with a trident and net. They banter until Finnick says it's lucky they're allies and shows her an identical wrist bangle to Haymitch's, which Katniss reads as an order to her to trust Finnick. She grudgingly agrees, but is immediately rewarded, when Finnick's command to duck and her swift response allows him to kill an attacker from District 5. He tells her not to trust Districts 1 and 2, and they agree to each take a side of the supply pile, but both find only weapons. Katniss fends off Enobaria with an arrow, catches Gloss in the calf with an arrow, grabs an extra bow and arrows, two knives, and an awl, and meets Finnick, who asks her to do something about Brutus running towards them. Brutus blocks her arrow with his belt, and rolls back into the water. Enobaria and Gloss reach the Cornucopia, and Katniss moves towards Peeta, still on his plate, with Finnick unquestioningly following her. Katniss starts to divest herself of weapons to swim out to him, but Finnick says he'll go because she shouldn't exert herself in her condition, which she had forgotten about. She is suspicious, but covers him as he brings Peeta to her. As they return, Katniss sees Mags dog paddling her way towards them—having figured out that the belts are flotation devices. Spotting Beetee at a distance, but not Wiress, and afraid Finnick might kill them, Katniss heads for the jungle with Peeta and the tributes from Districts 4. After hiking uphill a mile, they pause to rest, and climbing a tree, Katniss sees that the bloodbath at the Cornucopia is in progress. Katniss decides it would be best to deal with Finnick immediately, so she comes down prepared to kill him, but he seems to have anticipated her and stands with his trident ready. Peeta deliberately moving between them as he asks how many are dead prevents a showdown. Katniss guesses six. Finnick mentions their need to be concealed when the others come hunting them in the night, leading Katniss to conclude that it would be premature to kill Finnick now. The immediate problem is finding a source of fresh water. As they crest the hill they've climbed away from the water, Katniss spots a chink and realizes that they've reached the end of the arena. She's just starting to cry out a warning, when Peeta's knife hits the force field as he's slashing some vines, and he's electrocuted.

68   *Catching Fire: A Teaching Guide*

Chapter 20

Search for Water; Tree Rat and Spile; Tolling Bells

Chapter 20, page 280

Vocabulary

props 280 leans for support
notch 281 slot to keep arrow in place
once in a blue moon 281 very rarely
hormones 282 compounds in the body that change w/ pregnancy, affecting mood
vexed 282 distressed
quizzical 282 questioning; puzzled
beaten to a pulp 283 beaten seriously
playing the __ card 283 mentioning something to evoke strong emotions
aberration 284 departure from the norm
reconstructed 284 rebuilt surgically
humid 286 wet
vantage point 286 position w/ fine view
spurt 286 sudden burst
symmetrical 287 the same on both sides
tufts 288 clumps w/ strands coming out
tread 288 footsteps
stealthily 288 secretly
lush 288 thriving; attractive, flourishing
mottled 289 spotted with different shades
protruding 289 sticking out
muzzle 289 long, projecting nose and jaws of an animal; snout
radius 290 distance from center of a circle to its perimeter
sizzle 290 hissing sound from cooking
leery 290 appropriately suspicious
gamey 291 w/ tangy flavor, like game
snuffling 291 sniffing
divulge 293 reveal
hardwood 293 trees like oak and beech
stifling 293 suffocating
spile 293 spigot to tap maple sap
sap 294 fluid in plant's circulation system
sinewy 294 tough and stringy
wrest 295 remove by force
tolling 295 ringing
blister 297 break out in local swellings caused by an irritant touching the skin

Journal and Discussion Questions

1. Do you find it believable that, having seen resuscitation, Katniss doesn't recognize it? Explain what you think Collins is trying to do. Does she succeed?
2. Assess the functioning of the alliance in this chapter. Who does what?
3. What do Peeta's first sentences upon regaining consciousness reveal about him?
4. What do you think Finnick is trying to figure out on p. 282 as he glances between Katniss and Peeta? Explain why you think as you do
5. Summarize how Katniss applies prior knowledge in this chapter or doesn't.

Summary

Peeta is unresponsive, but Finnick resuscitates him. Katniss bursts into sobs, at least partly because now she can't imagine how she will be able to kill Finnick. Noticing Peeta's token, she sees it has a mockingjay and is concerned it will anger President Snow. The group agrees to move on slowly, with Katniss in the lead. Katniss is afraid that if she tells how she can identify the force field, the Gamemakers will alter it so she can't see the "chink," so she pretends she can hear it with her repaired left ear. Katniss ponders why Haymitch wanted her to ally with Finnick and why Finnick chose to save Peeta, as she tries to lead the group away from the center. But the force field curves inwards. She climbs a tree and discovers that the arena is a small, symmetrical pie-shape with the Cornucopia at the center and a force field above, as well as around the edges, and no water in sight besides the saltwater lake. Finnick chooses a camp near the force field, and he and Mags weave plants, while Peeta collects nuts that Mags has eaten without ill effect, and Katniss stands guard and then hunts for water. Hearing the eight cannon shots signaling eight victor deaths, she feels weak and sinks to the ground, catching sight of a rodent, which she shoots to get a better look. Its face is wet, but she can't find its water source, so she returns to the others, finding that they've created a hut and bowls. Peeta figures out how to cook using the force field, so they have "tree rat" and nuts for their first meal. They gather in the hut and wait for the recap, which reveals that all tributes in Districts 1–4 are alive, and Seeder and Cecilia, are dead. A silver parachute arrives with an object they can't initially identify, but as Katniss thinks of home, she realizes that it's a spile, and they realize the trees must be the water source. Finnick takes the first watch, and Katniss expects him to wake her, but is wakened instead by 12 tolls of a bell, which precede a bolt of lightning in the distance, followed by a storm. Katniss takes the watch and notices that the lightning storm stops after about an hour and then comes rain, which she can hear, but doesn't reach her group. She hears a cannon just before the rain suddenly stops all at once, reminding her of the storm in the previous Games. The fog that slides in, which she thinks at first is a natural response to the rain, is uniform, therefore Gamemaker-caused, and the smell confirms something is wrong, so she shouts to wake the others as her skin begins to blister.

Chapter 21

Fog and Monkeys; Death of Mags

Vocabulary

evade 299 hide from
debiltating 299 making it hard to function
spastic 300 jerking
surety 301 conviction; certainty
muster 301 bring to bear; show
contortions 301 unnatural twisting
prone 302 lying face down
abstract 302 disconnected from reality
vacuumed 303 sucked up
feat 303 performance
perforated 304 holey
purge 304 remove the poison from
sinuses 304 cavities behind the nose
functional 304 restored; fit

detoxify 305 remove the poison from
grimace 305 contorted expression
immersed 305 completely submerged
droplets 306 tiny drops
mere 308 nothing more than
irregularity 308 unexpected situation
dart 308 glance
converge on 308 come from all directions
hackles 308 hairs on back of animal's neck
switchblades 309 pocket knives w/ springs for quick release of blades
trajectory 310 planned path
skeletal 311 so thin that bones show plainly

Journal and Discussion Questions

1. How is Katniss's relationship to what's outside the arena different than in *HG*?
2. What is Mags's motivation for walking into the fog? Explain why you think this.
3. What do you think keeps the fog from continuing to move forward?
4. How does the effect of saltwater parallel an antidote in *The Hunger Games*?
5. Summarize the challenges the arena set-up has presented so far for the victors.

Summary

Screaming for her allies to run, Katniss rouses them. Finnick spots the fog, grabs Mags and heads off, but Peeta is not alert and not recovered, and Katniss has to explain that the fog contains poisonous gas and guide him, Peeta trips continually, but pushing away her impulse to save herself, Katniss guides him, following the calls of Finnick, who had stopped when he realized they were falling behind. When Peeta trips again, Katniss notices that the left side of his face is sagging, only to feel spasms in her arm and understand that the fog contains nerve gas. As Peeta's walk becomes spastic, Finnick returns and realizes that he'll have to carry Peeta, so he asks Katniss to carry Mags, and they set off again, with Finnick leading them at a diagonal so that they're heading towards the water. Katniss feels thankful she didn't kill Finnick. Then Katniss's right leg starts going stiff, causing her to fall repeatedly. She asks if Finnick can take both Mags and Peeta, but he can't because his arms aren't working. He apologizes to Mags, who kisses him and walks directly into the fog. Katniss's throat is burning so badly, she can't scream, and she drags herself after Finnick, who has already started away. Finally, Finnick falls, and Katniss falls over him and Peeta. When Katniss tries to rise in response to Finnick's groan, she sees the fog becoming thick, as if it's reached a transparent partition, and then disappear, as if it were being vacuumed away. A few minutes later, Peeta notices monkeys, and they all crawl down to the beach. The phrase "rubbing salt in a wound" takes on new meaning to Katniss when she feels the burning sensation of the saltwater, but she also sees that it is leaching out the poison. She strips off her jumpsuit, which has been seriously damaged by the fog, and finds that her undergarments, shoes, and belt are unaffected. She notices that Peeta seems to be using the saltwater as she is, but Finnick is lying in the sand. Katniss and Peeta bring water to him, until Katniss realizes how vulnerable they are to attack, and she and Peeta take a leg each, drag him into the water, and give him a controlled soaking until he is able to duck his head under himself. Peeta goes to drill a hole to get them water, using a knife, since the awl is gone. Katniss ponders why Finnick abandoned Mags for Peeta and why Mags accepted this and walked into the fog, but Finnick's expression keeps her from asking. They go to help Peeta and spot scores of monkeys that seem ominous. Preparing for battle, Katniss calls to Peeta to join them, trying to express urgency but avoid panic, and though Peeta catches her tone and moves casually, he makes eye contact with a monkey above him, which initiates an attack, making it clear that they are muttations. Katniss runs out of arrows and shouts to Peeta for his, when a monkey leaps for his chest. Finnick, who has just speared another monkey, cannot help him, and the mutt evades the knife Katniss throws. She runs to cover him with her body, even though she knows she can't get there in time, when the female morphling from District 6 jumps out of nowhere, it seems, into the mutt's path and takes its fangs in her chest, saving Peeta's life.

70 *Catching Fire: A Teaching Guide*

Chapter 22

Johanna Joins Alliance with Beetee and Wiress

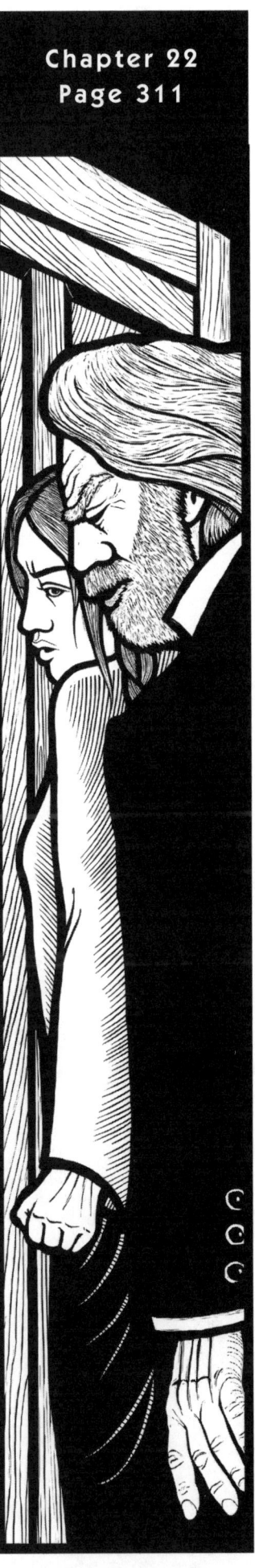

Chapter 22
Page 311

Vocabulary

ruptured 312 burst
vacant look 312 unfocused gaze
shimmers 312 shines with flickering light
dabbles 312 playfully splashes
entranced 313 completely absorbed in; totally focused on
dappled 313 spotted
pronged 313 w/ sharp, projecting points
gore 313 blood
marred 314 damaged
slake 314 quench; satisfy
plunk 315 sit down heavily
tar 315 substance made from coal and used to treat skin conditions
glob 316 small, rounded, semi-liquid mass
ghastly 316 shocking
decomposing 316 rotting; disintegrating
slather 316 spread thickly
singsong 316 w/ a monotonous rise and fall of pitch
disdainful 317 scornful; contemptuous
deranged 319 mentally unstable; insane
grouchily 319 in a complaining way; grumpily
counterpart 320 one of two that make a whole
careens 320 rushes into; tips over into
writhing 320 twisting; struggling
pallor 321 unhealthy paleness
epidemic 322 outbreak of contagious illness
dilated 322 widened
drag 324 weight that slows forward progress
under my breath 325 in a very quiet voice, not meant to carry (or be heard)

Journal and Discussion Questions

1. Identify the sacrifices that have occurred in the series so far.
2. What do you make of Katniss's request and how quickly the parachute arrives?
3. What do you gather from the joke Finnick and Katniss play on Peeta?.
4. What conclusions have you drawn about Johanna's motivation? What evidence supports your conclusions?
5. List the evidence Katniss uses to draw the conclusion that the arena is a clock.
6. What is the important detail that Finnick fails to mention in recounting the alliances adventures so far? Why do you think he omitted it?
7. What do you make of the various victors' choices that keep Peeta alive? Use the Choice Tool to analyze them as deeply as you can, given the limitations of seeing into their thoughts only through Katniss's first-person narration.
8. Write a possible ending for *Catching Fire* in which you pick up after Chapter 22 ends on p. 325. Do not look ahead in the book as you do this. (Obviously, if you have read the story already or have seen the movie, this will be a different type of exercise for you. In this case, you will attempt to write an alternative ending that works.) Be sure to identify elements of the story that need to be settled because they've been foreshadowed, or because the plot has created an open question. For example, we would expect to learn the outcome of the Quarter Quell. Also, be sure to note items that should remain open to be dealt with in the final volume. For example, since the title of the third book is *Mockingjay*, we would expect that whatever the main conflict is will somehow relate to the symbolism set up for the mockingjay in *Catching Fire*. These are just a few of the items that should be addressed.
9. Summarize the times in the series so far when you know or suspect Peeta has intentionally used his abilities to speak engagingly and persuasively and the effects of his speech in each case.

Summary

Peeta stabs the monkey to death, while Katniss—now rearmed—braces for another barrage, but the monkeys fade into the jungle as if the Gamemakers were recalling them. Katniss and Finnick cover Peeta as he carries the morphling to the beach and sets her down. It is clear that she is dying. Finnick walks away to guard along the tree line, but the morphling grips Katniss's hand so tightly that she feels she has to stay. Peeta strokes the morphling's hair and gently talks to her of colors, because she loved to paint. She dabbles in the blood on her chest and uses it to paint on Peeta's cheek, and when he thanks her, she dies. Peeta carries her out into the water, and she's picked up by a hovercraft.

Chapter 22, cont.

Finnick recovers Katniss's arrows, and Katniss sets about cleaning them, noticing that the spots where the fog had burned her are now scabbed over and enormously itchy. She sees that Finnick and Peeta are both scratching their faces. They again attempt to get water, this time without interruption. Katniss suggests that the men sleep while she watches, but Finnick says he'd rather, and Katniss realizes he wants privacy to mourn Mags. Katniss awakes to find that Finnick has constructed a shelter to shield them from the sun, as well as created three bowls, two filled with water and one with shellfish. She goes to the water to wash her hands prior to eating, and as she come back up the beach, she shouts to Haymitch that if he's not too drunk, they could use something for their skin, and a parachute immediately floats into view: the thick dark ointment it contains looks awful, but relieves the itching and also seems to be a sunblock. Finnick suggests they stick their grotesque looking faces into Peeta's to wake him, and Peeta's shock amuses them. Immediately, there's a parachute with a loaf of District 4 bread, which Katniss takes to mean that if she's friendly with Finnick, she'll get food.

Katniss reviews in her mind that 11 tributes are dead and 13 are alive. She doesn't "really feel like" trying to remember who is left beside the Careers. For the moment, there is an unspoken agreement to stick to the beach. Then they hear screams and see a gigantic wave crest on the hill across from them and rush down the slope to the water around the Cornucopia, sending a tide up to where Katniss's group is sitting. A cannon fires, indicating they're down to 12 living victors, and Katniss spots three victors about two spokes' distance away, one being dragged, one wandering in circles, and one really angry. Finnick recognizes Johanna and runs towards her, with Peeta and Katniss following, figuring they can't leave him. But Katniss has serious reservations about Johanna.

As they draw near, Katniss sees that the other two are Wiress and Beetee, and when they come up to the group, Johanna is describing a rain of blood that they were trying to escape when Johanna's male counterpart from District 7 ran into the force field. She explains that Beetee got knifed in the back at the Cornucopia and Wiress is in shock, saying, "Tick, tock" repeatedly, which Wiress begins again on cue, causing Johanna to shove her, and Katniss to tell Johanna to lay off. Johanna begins to yell about getting them out of the jungle for Katniss, when Finnick picks her up and dunks her repeatedly in the water, while Katniss asks Peeta what Johanna meant about getting them for her.

Recognizing how badly off Beetee is, Katniss and Peeta leave Wiress to wash up—though she just sits and mumbles "Tick, tock"—and clean Beetee, taking care of his wound as best they can, tying moss to his back to staunch the bleeding. Leaving Beetee in the shade, after getting him some water, Katniss returns to Wiress, who seems terrified. She is clearly trying to communicate something by saying, "Tick, tock," but Katniss can't understand her without Beetee. Finnick and Johanna rejoin them, and Johanna eats, while Katniss tries to get Wiress to eat, and Finnick tells about the fog and the monkeys, but leaving out "the most important detail."

Johanna and Katniss take the first guard shift, and Johanna asks how Mags was lost. When Katniss tells her. Johanna tells her accusatorily that Mags was Finnick's mentor and half his family, and Katniss responds that she didn't know. Katniss asks what Johanna was doing with Beetee and Wiress, and Johanna expands on what she previously said, explaining that Haymitch said that if Johanna wanted to be allies she had to bring them to Katniss, and asking Katniss to verify that this is what she told Haymitch, to which Katniss mentally replies, "no," though out loud she thanks Johanna. Wiress wanders over, still saying, "Tick, tock," prompting Johanna to go away to sleep. As Katniss tries to calm Wiress, she notes the position of the sun, indicating noon, and then recalls the 12 tolls of the bell, as if for midnight, looks at the pie shape wedges, identifies the "plague" that belongs to the ones she's experienced, and realizes what Wiress is trying to say: that the arena is a clock.

Chapter 23

Figuring Out the Clock; Spinning Island

Chapter 23
Page 326

Vocabulary

congealed 328 solidified
garrote 328 material used for strangling
garroting 328 strangling with a garrote
intuitive 330 having strong, accurate instincts or intuitions
toddle 331 walk with short, unsteady steps
centrifugal 333 moving away from center
unstable 333 not steady; wobbling
deceleration 333 slowing down
borne 334 held up; supported

waterlogged 334 filled w/ water
articulated 336 explained
scrutinizing 336 looking carefully at
gut feeling 336 intuition
decipher 336 figure out
uneasy 337 troubling; unsettling
unfathomable 337 impossible to grasp
subvert 338 overthrow; undermine
underlying 338 basic; fundamental
heedless of 339 w/out considering; despite

Journal and Discussion Questions

1. Katniss chose not to explain the chink in the force field because of the Gamemakers (p. 284). Why does she explain the clock, without considering them?
2. What does Katniss mean when she says, "Or maybe this had been the plan all along" (p. 327)?
3. What song does Wiress sing? Why doesn't Katniss recognize it?
4. How does Katniss deal with the horrible choices facing her?
5. What detail reveals that Beetee knows things about districts beyond his own?
6. Summarize the chapter from Finnick's point of view.

Summary

Katniss grasps the clock arrangement and realizes they must move, explaining the theory in a way that convinces everybody but Johanna, and confirming to Wiress that her warning has worked. When Wiress mentions midnight, Katniss responds, "It starts at midnight," leading her to recall Plutarch's words at the dinner and realize that he was giving her a clue, without understanding why. Wiress, now eats and drinks. Beetee is conscious, but calling for his wire, which Johanna identifies as a cylinder of coiled wire, though she doesn't recognize it as his weapon of choice that he used to win the Games, which makes Katniss question Johanna suspiciously. Johanna responds angrily, and Katniss concludes that, sooner or later, one of them will kill the other. Finnick suggests they all watch their steps and gives Beetee the wire. Peeta picks Beetee up, and Finnick suggests they watch from the Cornucopia. As they move, Katniss considers what will happen to winnow the allies down to just Peeta. She figures Beetee and Wiress will die on their own, and she'll kill Johanna. But with all she owes Finnick, she can't imagine killing him, so instead she fantasizes about killing President Snow. At the Cornucopia, Peeta puts Beetee in the shade. Wiress goes into the water to clean the coil of wire, noting that it is two o'clock when the fog starts. Beetee explains that she is intuitive and similar to the canary in the mines. Johanna picks two axes out of the remaining pile of weapons, while Peeta draws a map of the arena on a leaf, noting the plagues they know of, until Katniss realizes that Wiress is silent, and seeing that Gloss has slit her throat, shoots him in the head, while Johanna kills Cashmere with an ax. Finnick protects Peeta from a spear thrown by Brutus, but gets knifed in the thigh by Enobaria, and the cannon sounds three times. As the allies start to chase Brutus and Enobaria, they are knocked to the ground by the spinning of the island. When it stops, Beetee and all three of the dead are in the water. Finnick swims out for Beetee, and Katniss, remembering the wire, swims out to Wiress despite the hovercraft, and rescues the wire, closes Wiress's eyelids, and says goodbye. The allies decide to head to 12 on the clock, but now realize that—with the Cornucopia spun—they no longer know where 12 is. Katniss regrets having mentioned the clock, and Beetee points out that the wave at 10 will help them identify where the segments are again. Johanna adds that Katniss had to explain it to convince them to move. They head for the outer rim, and Peeta proposes to tap a tree, but Finnick says it's his turn, and when Peeta offers to guard, Johanna says Katniss should while Peeta reconstructs the map, since the original washed away. Katniss is suspicious that this is an attempt to divide her from Peeta, but goes anyway. She feels uneasy as she recalls all the sacrifices other victors have made for Peeta, but concludes that Haymitch has persuaded everyone that Peeta's ability to convince others would provide the greatest threat to the Capitol, and they agreed to sacrifice themselves for him. Finnick calls to her for the spile, but as she hands it to him, she hears Prim scream and dashes into the jungle to protect her.

Chapter 24
Page 340

Chapter 24

Jabberjay Attack; Peeta's Locket

Vocabulary

irretrievable 340 unable to be restored
forerunner 341 ancestor
fuse 341 MM combine
instantaneous 341 immediate
rational 341 reasoned; logical
gutsy 347 courageous; daring
configuration 349 pattern; arrangement
recede 350 flow back
theoretically 350 in principle
confines 350 limits

double deal 351 appearance of following one path while secretly following another; agreeing to two, mutually exclusive plans
inhabited 353 experienced
arsenal 353 collection of weapons (fig.)
absurdity 355 impossibility
cling 355 hold onto; consider (mentally)
descent 355 lowering
working at cross-purposes 356 aiming at goals that conflict

Journal and Discussion Questions

1. Compare and contrast the Capitol's use of jabberjays in the arena and the wild.
2. What might have happened if only one victor were trapped with the jabberjays?
3. Explain the ellipses on p. 342 when Katniss says, "It's not your . . . ."
4. Twice in this chapter, Peeta works to persuade others. Do you think he believes everything he says? Offer evidence to support your conclusions.
5. Summarize the time in the arena so far by imagining Capitol residents blow-by-blow reactions to events.

Summary

Katniss runs after "Prim"—who sounds both desperately hurt and just out of reach—until she spots a jabberjay and recognizes a Gamemaker trick. Finnick arrives, but her explanation is interrupted by the shrieks of a young woman, and Finnick runs off in pursuit. Katniss catches up as he is circling a tree, calling for *Annie*. Unable to get his attention, she scales a neighboring tree and shoots the jabberjay, which falls at his feet. He is not consoled because he believes Annie (and Prim) were tortured to create the cries that the jabberjays reproduce. Katniss sinks to the ground, and the next bird starts with Gale's voice. Finnick prevents Katniss from chasing it and tries to lead her out of the wedge. Eventually, Katniss cooperates. When she spots Peeta and Johanna, she is relieved, but angry that they didn't come to help, until she and Finnick run into a transparent wall that encloses the wedge. More jabberjays arrive, and Katniss shoots them till she has no arrows left, and then joins Finnick crouched on the ground, ears covered. Peeta's touch tells her it's over, and he attempts to convince them that Prim and Annie weren't actually tortured because the Capitol needs to interview them all when there are only eight tributes left. Beetee confirms that a recording could be altered, and Johanna points out that the there would be an uprising if anything happened to Prim, and then yells about the whole country being in rebellion, causing Katniss to admire her courage. Johanna goes to get water, and despite the birds being gone, Katniss tries to stop her so she won't be tortured by cries of loved ones, but Johanna says there's no one left whom she loves. Peeta infers that Annie is Annie Cresta, the girl for whom Mags volunteered and who won five years earlier, though the experience drove her mad. A cannon blast sounds, and they see an unidentifiable person retrieved in five separate segments. Now that they know their location, Peeta draws a new map, adding the jabberjay segment and "beast" where the dismembered tribute died. District 2 tributes and Chaff are still alive. A parachute arrives with 24 rolls from District 3, and they each have three and save the rest. After the wave, they head to that section because they are theoretically safe for 12 hours. Peeta and Katniss take the first watch, and Peeta tells Katniss that they know each other's motivations, and that Haymitch must have lied to one of them in the promises he made. He reminds Katniss that while she could have a worthwhile life after the Games, he has nothing to live for besides her. He reveals that his token is a locket with a photo of Mrs. Everdeen and Prim on one side and Gale on the other, making his intentions clear. That he doesn't mention the (pretend) baby convinces her that his speech is not part of the Games. Peeta adds that no one truly needs him, and Katniss realizes that she does and says so, upsetting Peeta, who is stopped from arguing by Katniss kissing him until the first strike of the lightning storm startles them apart and wakes Finnick. Finnick comes to take the watch from one of them, and Peeta puts the locket chain around Katniss's neck, places his hand on her stomach, and tells her that she's going to make a great mother, signaling a return to "Gamespeak." Katniss tries to imagine a world that would be safe for Peeta's child as she falls asleep.

74   *Catching Fire: A Teaching Guide*

Strategy 18

Assessing Various Types of Persuasion

Persuasive discourse attempts to change what the audience thinks, feels, believes, or values, or to move the audience to take action. In most persuasive discourse, the writer or speaker states a position and provides evidence or reasons that attempt to convince the audience to embrace that position. Look back at the section of Chapter 24 that begins with Peeta telling Katniss that "it's no use pretending we don't know what the other one is trying to do" (p. 350). This speech is an example of persuasion.

Writers and speakers use various techniques to make their communications persuasive. Some of these techniques are accepted in our culture in both formal and informal situations as examples of convincing argument. Other techniques are frowned upon because they are unacceptable for some reason. Here are some commonly used techniques that are considered valid in the real world and in the United States.

- **Appeal to reason.** If something makes good sense, that in itself can be convincing. Telling your audience what benefits they would derive from following your advice can be helpful.
- **Appeal to authority.** Use this technique as a way to substantiate your claims. Make sure that the authority you cite is well respected. Usually when we talk about appealing to authority we mean a well-respected person or authoritative print or digital source, but the authority of experience can also carry a great deal of weight.
- **Appeal to a principle, belief, or ideal that you and your audience share.** Finding common ground is helpful in persuading others.
- **Using specific details.** This includes statistics and other numerical data. If you use numbers or other facts, verify them carefully. You have a responsibility to present accurate information.

But the lines are drawn differently in Panem as a whole and in the arena in particular. **Appeals to force** or **threats** are a type of persuasion that is often criminal in our culture, but is frequently used successfully by the Capitol. Certain argument techniques that are not criminal are still considered unacceptable in our culture, but are highly successful in the arena, like **appeals to the audience's prejudices**, **appeals to base instincts** (like greed), or **appeals to the audience's emotions** divorced from logic and reason. These appeals are valuable in the Games when one's potential sponsors are watching for the vicarious thrill they get from sentiment, on the one hand, and death, on the other. Not all persuasive techniques are used consciously—for example, Katniss is able to persuade others by who she is and her **charisma**, but "She has no idea. The effect she can have" (*HG* p. 91). As you read works set in other times, cultures, and worlds, keep an eye on how persuasion works and what's acceptable.

1. List five situations in *Catching Fire* in which Katniss has attempted to persuade someone. Did she succeed?
2. For each of the 9 persuasive techniques mentioned (appeal to reason; appeal to authority; appeal to a principle, belief, or ideal that you and your audience share; using specific details; appeal to force; appeal to prejudices; appeal to base instincts; appeal to emotions; and charisma) locate instances in the *Hunger Games* trilogy so far in which the techniques were used and record the words from the book.

Directions: First, read the information. Then, answer the question or questions.

Chapter 25   Beetee's Plan

Vocabulary

proposition 357 proposal; suggestion; plan
excluded 358 kept out
shoos 358 waves arms as a signal to back off
conductive 359 able to transmit electrical current
component 360 element; ingredient
harnessing 360 taking control of
dispute 361 argue against
disconcerted 361 perturbed; confused
muggy 362 warm and very humid
weighs on 362 is a burden to
sector 363 wedge in the arena "clock"
pincers 364 grasping claws that open and close like a hinge
encompasses 364 surrounds
sliminess 365 quality of being moist, soft, and slippery
supplements 366 additions
succulent 366 juicy

Journal and Discussion Questions

1. What do you think is the significance of Katniss's happiness upon awakening?
2. What do you make of the gifts sent via parachute so far in the Quarter Quell?
3. When Katniss wants to speak privately to Peeta, what are her concerns?
4. Offer another explanation besides the one Beetee gives for why the last fight between the allies and the District 2 tributes ended as it did.
5. Compare and contrast Peeta's technique for convincing Katniss and Finnick that the jabberjays' sounds do not mean that Prim and Annie have actually been hurt with Beetee's technique for convincing the allies that his plan is worth following. What similarities and differences do you discover?
6. What has changed in the relationships between the allies since Chapter 22?
7. Do you think Beetee's trap will work? Explain why you think as you do, in terms of science, evidence in the text, and the plot development of the trilogy.
8. What revelation does Peeta have after giving Katniss the pearl?
9. How does Katniss deal with what she expects to be her future?
10. Summarize the loose ends you see in need of tying up.

Summary

Katniss awakens momentarily happy, a feeling quickly dissipated by her surroundings. A parachute descends, again carrying 24 of the rolls from District 3. They divide them and the leftovers from the previous evening, leaving eight. Katniss questions how long the alliance can endure, especially with Katniss unsure about the others' motivation for and commitment to protecting Peeta. She decides it's time for her and Peeta to separate themselves, and under the pretense of teaching Peeta to swim and showing him how a light rubbing with sand removes the itchy scabs, she proposes they end the alliance. He counters that they should stay until Brutus and Enobaria are dead because he thinks Beetee is creating a trap for them. Reminding herself that she must make decisions based solely on Peeta's survival, Katniss agrees in order to avoid having to face two sets of enemies, and calls Finnick to join them in scouring off his scabs.

Beetee calls them over and enunciates what he takes to be the next priority, which is to kill Brutus and Enobaria. He leads them through what he believes the Careers will have surmised about the arena, and proposes a trap. Drawing a rough diagram of the arena, he leads the group to understand that Brutus and Enobaria aren't in the safest part of the arena (where they, themselves, are) both because they are outnumbered and because the spot is occupied. He therefore proposes that they leave the beach and run his wire from the lightning bolt tree to the water. This will make the beach inviting for Brutus and Enobaria, but when lightning strikes, electricity will run down the wire, electrocuting anyone in the water or on the beach, which will be still damp from the wave at that time.

Questioned by Johanna, Beetee reveals that he knows how the wire works because he invented it, and adds that neither the lightning nor the tree are "real." Katniss points out that the Careers will be safe unless they're close enough to the target area, and Peeta notes that the seafood will be cooked, eliminating a source of food. Beetee agrees with both of them, but reminds them of the nuts and rats that the original allies had found in the jungle. Declaring that everyone's cooperation will be needed to make the plan work, Beetee opens it up to their vote. But—as Katniss notes—none of them (all

76   *Catching Fire: A Teaching Guide*

from districts other than 3) are in no position to dispute his scientific claims. Katniss suggests that if it works, there's a good chance of eliminating the Careers, and if it doesn't, the Careers will also lose a food source. Peeta agrees, but Finnick waits for Johanna to agree before he does.

Beetee wants to look over the lightning tree, so they head up into the jungle, with Katniss wishing Haymitch would send the saltier District 4 bread. Johanna leads and Katniss guards the rear. When they get close to the force field, Finnick suggests Katniss lead, saying she can hear it. Beetee seems surprised, but doesn't contradict her, and she uses the nuts, as before, sees the chink, and warns the others to stay downhill from the lightning tree. Beetee examines the tree, with Finnick standing guard, Johanna drilling for water, Peeta gathering nuts, and Katniss hunting. Then Peeta and Katniss roast nuts and cook tree rat meat. The group moves away to avoid the lightning strike, watches the results, and then heads back to the 10 o'clock beach. There, Beetee works with his wire, while the others nap and then prepare their last seafood feast. Peeta finds a pearl and gives it to Katniss, who thanks him, even as she privately reconfirms her intention to insure that his plan doesn't work. Peeta can see this in her face, and asks her about the effect of the locket, even though the others are present. She says it worked, but he realizes it was not the way he meant it to work. As they prepare to eat, a parachute comes with spicy red sauce and another 24 rolls from District 3, making 32 rolls, from which they each take five, leaving seven. They stuff themselves and throw the leftover seafood into the water so it won't feed the Careers. Peeta and Katniss sit together, silent. She has secured the pearl, the spile, and the medicine in a parachute at her waist, and she hopes that it is returned to District 12 with her body and that her mother and Prim give the pearl back to Peeta before they bury her.

Chapter 25, cont.

Writer's Forum 6

Writing Instructions or Directions

The purpose of writing **instructions** or **directions** is either to explain to your audience how a process works or, more often, to enable them to actually carry out the process. Because it usually has a practical aim, this type of writing has to be clear, accurate, and (often) detailed.

Achieving clarity, accuracy, and the necessary level of detail means knowing the process well yourself or having excellent sources that you can derive your understanding from in order to pass it on. You also need to accurately assess your audience's understanding and prior knowledge in order to give your instructions in a way that they will understand.

Since order is often critical in instructions, it is always useful to use words that identify sequence and relationship in time, such as those in the following list:

after that	first, second . . .	previously
afterwards	following	prior to
all the while	history	simultaneously
as soon as	if . . . then	since
at the same time	immediately	soon
because	in the meantime	subsequently
before	last	then
cause	later	therefore
consequently	meanwhile	to begin with
earlier	next	until
effect	now	when
finally	once	while

These words help clarify things that happen before, after, and during other occurrences, how close in time they are/do/should occur, and causal relationships between elements in the instructions (e.g., yeast causes dough to rise). The last category points to another aspect of instructions: to explain how something works and why it works while directing someone about how to do it.

Instructions are always given in time order, and often have a list of materials or ingredients. A list of materials or ingredients serves several purposes. The most obvious use is that it allows the person following the instructions to quickly and easily identify whether s/he has all of the necessary items to complete the project. But beyond that, a good materials list will allow the person to identify any tasks that need to be done prior to starting the first step listed. If the list specifies a "smooth board" and the only board available is rough and splintery, then the person can figure that—in his or her case—there is an added initial step that must be taken prior to beginning the instructions as written.

1. Write instructions for Beetee's plan, reorganizing the information in Chapter 25 as needed. Your instructions should differ from ordinary instructions in that whenever you are unclear about how, when, or why something is to be done, you should include a note to that effect. For example, you might write, "The next step is to ___, but it's unclear why you would want to do this."

2. Upon completion of 1, use your instructions to assess Collins's narration of Beetee's instructions for clarity. What do you make of how she chose to present Beetee's plan?

Directions:
First, read the information. Then, answer the question or questions.

Chapter 26

Johanna Attacks Katniss; Katniss Completes Beetee's Plan

Chapter 26, Page 368

Vocabulary

erupts 369 becomes violently active
aftermath 369 secondary results
sure-footed 369 unlikely to fall or stumble
pretty good clip 370 fairly fast pace
manning 370 being in charge of
miscalculated 370 estimated or figured incorrectly
slack 372 loose; not taut
snags 374 gets tangled
surging 375 rushing
festooned 375 wrapped in as if decorated with garlands
involuntary 375 made without conscious choice or control
squint 376 narrow the eyes in an effort to improve vision
falter 376 become unsteady; lose its effectiveness
bristle 378 show annoyance
paralyzed 379 unable to move

Journal and Discussion Questions

1. Chart Katniss's references to the audience and sponsors in the arena for the Quarter Quell. Then tell what you think is responsible for the change from *HG*.
2. Assess Katniss's hypotheses about what has happened after her arm is cut. Do they seem reasonable based on what she knows?
3. What do you think happened to Beetee? Explain why you think as you do.
4. Whom do you think Katniss identified as the enemy? What evidence supports your answer?
5. Predict what will happen in Chapter 27.
6. Summarize the chapter based on your own conjectures, even if they differ from Katniss's.

Summary

The anthem begins to play, but there are no deaths to report. Katniss is sure the audience will be wanting more deaths, but thinks that the Gamemakers are holding off because Beetee's trap may provide them without their interference. At approximately nine p.m., they head for the 12 o'clock beach and start the hike up to the lightning tree. At the tree, Beetee unwinds some wire that he sets aside before he has Finnick help him wrap wire around the tree in a particular pattern. They finish as they hear the wave at about 10:30 p.m.

Beetee explains that Johanna and Katniss are to take the coil down to the beach, unwinding as they go—one unwrapping the spool, the other guarding—and dropping the spool into the water at the end. Peeta wants to go with, but Beetee says he needs Peeta and that there's no time to debate if the women are to get to safety before the lightning strikes. Beetee directs Katniss and Johanna to head for the tree in the 1 o'clock to 2 o'clock section or even the next section, if they're running out of time. They start off with Johanna unwrapping the wire and Katniss guarding, and they are in the process of switching when the wire falls from higher up the hill and bunches around their feet. Katniss figures someone has cut the wire, and as she lets go of the cylinder to arm an arrow, Johanna smashes the cylinder into her head, knocking her onto her back, sits on her chest, and digs into her left forearm with a knife. She then wipes blood from Katniss's arm onto her face and hisses at Katniss to stay down, but Katniss is having trouble construing things, and remembers that Johanna said the same thing to Wiress.

Katniss hears footsteps and then hears Brutus say to Enobaria that Katniss is as good as dead, and she wonders if this is true as she drifts in and out of consciousness. Katniss assumes, without examining her arm, that Johanna has done irreparable damage to her and was interrupted in her murderous attack by the Careers showing up. She concludes that the alliance is over and that Finnick and Johanna must have had an agreement to attack Peeta and Katniss this evening. She's not sure where Beetee fits in. Thinking of Peeta, she is able to work out that the wire having been cut by the Careers near where Katniss and Johanna were, Beetee, Finnick, and Peeta will not know what has happened, although they probably guessed something from changes to the wire. She figures Johanna will bring Finnick into the fight as soon as she's free of the Careers, so Katniss must get to Peeta as quickly as possible, though dizziness makes it hard for her to even sit up.

Because her arm starts squirting blood when she raises it, Katniss bandages her forearm with moss, but without examining the wound. She touches her head wound and finds a lump, but little blood. She arms her bow and heads up the slope, going over

Catching Fire: A Teaching Guide 79

Chapter 26, cont.

reasons why she should no longer trust Finnick just as someone comes running down towards her, causing her to hide. She sees Finnick and hears him call her and Johanna and then move off in the same direction Johanna and the Careers went in. She tries to listen, but the insects interfere. She begins to run when she hears a cannon until her feet are caught in what she first believes to be a net made by Finnick and then realizes is more of the wire. When she sees the lightning tree, she risks calling Peeta's name softly, but is answered by a groan from Beetee who has a gash below his elbow. He cannot speak, but Katniss sees that he is holding one of Peeta's knives attached to the length of wire that he left on the ground before he and Finnick started winding the tree. Katniss wonders if Beetee tried to drive the knife into the force field, possibly as a backup plan. Katniss hears Peeta call her. She realizes that she can't protect him, but she can draw the attackers away from him, so she yells, and she hears two of them crashing towards her. Sinking to the ground by Beetee—she aims an arrow in the direction of the two approaching tributes, who turn out to be Enobaria and Finnick.

Katniss aims at Enobaria's neck as the insect sounds die out, knowing she can kill them both and leave Peeta with only one enemy. The word *enemy* brings Haymitch's last words to her to mind, and she realizes that Enobaria is not the enemy and understands the purpose of Beetee's knife. She slides the wire off the knife, wraps and secures it to an arrow and shoots it into the chink in the force field, causing a flash of light. Katniss falls to the ground paralyzed, but with her eyes open, as a series of explosions begins.

Chapter 27

Rescue of the Tributes; The Rebellion Begins

Vocabulary

bombardment 381 rapid, continuous, very loud sounds
fervently 381 deeply; w/ great emotion
flipper 382 limb without fingers
semiconsciousness 382 in a state between full consciousness and being blacked out
motor coordination 382 ability to control one's movements
ajar 383 open
full-scale 385 complete; all-out
indiscretion 386 action that revealed something meant to be secret
magnitude 387 importance
subterfuges 387 deceptions; strategic tricks used to conceal
gone right off the deep end 388 become insane
entreaties 390 pleas
deathblow 391 information that destroys cherished hopes

Journal and Discussion Questions

1. What is the first clue in the chapter that Katniss has completely misunderstood her situation? Explain.
2. Why does Plutarch close Katniss's eyes? What evidence supports your view?
3. Why do you think Haymitch's explanation is summarized by Katniss rather than given in Haymitch's own voice?
4. Match up the districts from the list Haymitch gives Katniss (p. 385) with the support she and Peeta receive and contributions to the break-out plan.
5. Why has Katniss come to consider Haymitch an enemy? Do you think her response is justified? Explain why you think as you do.
6. What causes Katniss to say she hates Peeta?
7. How is Katniss's response to Gale different from her response to everyone else?
8. In what ways would you imagine Gale's perspective on what has happened to Katniss would be similar to and different from Katniss's own views?
9. Summarize the chapter from Haymitch's point of view.
10 Summarize the novel by either: a) drawing an image to represent each chapter or b) creating a title for each chapter to capture its contents.

Summary

Katniss witnesses a series of explosions of earth and sky and then realizes that there are fireworks going off. She wonders if there will be any victor to the Quarter Quell and whether the intention all along was to kill all the tributes. In her mind, she apologizes to Peeta for not saving him and wonders if she condemned him by destroying the force field. She sees a hovercraft above her, and realizes that the din had drowned out its sound. The claw drops down and lifts her up, and she is powerless to stop it. Seeing Plutarch when she is brought inside, and feeling him close her eyes, she hopes that the wound in her forearm will kill her.

When she regains consciousness, she is lying on a padded table with tubes in her left arm. Her right arm has some movement, enabling her to clumsily rip out the tubes, which sets off beeping, the results of which she does not see because she loses consciousness again. When she next awakens, her hands are tied down, but by lifting her head, she can see other beds and hear Beetee—who has a bunch of machines hooked to him—breathing. Wishing those who hold her prisoner would just let her die, she slams her head on the table until she loses consciousness. Finally, she awakens to find herself in control of her body and unrestrained. She sees only Beetee in the room, and wonders what happened to the others. Since she failed to save Peeta she intends to keep him safe from the Capitol by killing him, and to this end, she grabs an empty syringe, passing up the chance to kill Beetee because that would set off alarms and prevent her from "saving" Peeta.

She heads down a hallway to a slightly open metal door, and listens, syringe in hand. She hears a report on the Districts from Plutarch and hears him telling Finnick that they can't take him to District 4. As Katniss tries to figure out people's motivations, she hears Haymitch speak, leading her to barge through the door and see that they are flying. Haymitch catches her to steady her, but makes her drop the syringe and puts her in a chair, telling her that her attempt to fight the Capitol with a syringe is an example of why she isn't allowed to know about plans.

Plutarch gives her soup and a roll, and Haymitch says he's going to explain and

Chapter 27, cont.

asks her not to speak until he's done. He tells her that as soon as the Quarter Quell was announced, a plan was put in development to break the tributes out, a plan which victors from Districts 3, 4, 6, 7, 8, and 11 each had some knowledge of. Plutarch, who has long been a member of a group aiming to overthrow the Capitol, ensured that Beetee had the wire he needed, and Beetee was tasked with blowing a hole in the force field. The bread was a code, with the district number signaling the number of the day in the arena and the number of rolls the hour of the day for the escape. The hovercraft was provided by District 13, which does, in fact, exist, and where they are headed, by a roundabout route, and most of Panem is in rebellion. Katniss's response is to feel that she's gone from being the Capitol's pawn to a pawn in this rebel plan.

When Katniss asks, Haymitch explains that she and Peeta weren't told because they would have been the Capitol's first targets for capture, and so it was better that they not know anything. Katniss asks why she and Peeta would be targeted, and Finnick answers that it is for the same reason that the rest of the victors agreed to die to keep Katniss and Peeta alive. Katniss protests that Johanna tried to kill her, and Haymitch explains that Johanna knocked her out to get the tracker out of her arm and to lead Brutus and Enobaria away. Plutarch then tells her that she had to be saved because she's the mockingjay, the symbol of the revolution, as she had suspected, though Haymitch's rejection of her plans to start an uprising threw her off the track. She whispers Peeta's name, and Haymitch explains that they knew that without Peeta, Katniss wouldn't enter an alliance. She demands to know where he is, and Haymitch confesses that the Capitol got Peeta, Johanna, and Enobaria, leading Katniss to attack Haymitch with her fingernails, while they both scream terrible things at each other, but Haymitch does not hurt her.

Finnick and others get hold of her and she is restrained and sedated, but not asleep. Their soothing words have no effect, nor do Finnick's apology and explanation that he wanted to go back for Peeta and Johanna but couldn't because he was paralyzed. Finnick goes on, speculating that because Peeta doesn't actually know anything, they won't torture him, and they'll keep him alive if they think they can use him against Katniss. Katniss asks if he means they'll use Peeta—and Annie—like bait, and ignores his weeping in response. Finnick says he wishes Annie, Peeta, Katniss, and he, himself, were all dead, because that would be better. Katniss stops to consider if she really wants Peeta dead and decides she really wants him back, but since she's sure she'll never get him back, dead is the next best option. Reflecting that Peeta may feel that he fulfilled his mission to keep her alive, Katniss decides she hates him even more than Haymitch. Katniss then gives up on life, refusing sustenance and imagining that if she dies perhaps Peeta will be allowed to live as an Avox, but even if not, dying of spite will punish Haymitch. She is able to ignore everyone who tries to talk to her until the day when she hears Gale's voice, and the thought of the others at home, whom she had forgotten, comes back to her. Gale assures her that Prim and her mother are alive, but not in District 12, which—he implies—has suffered the same fate as the Hob. Despite her indications that she's not prepared for the news, Gale tells Katniss that there is no longer a District 12.

82 *Catching Fire: A Teaching Guide*

Strategy 19

Understanding Logical Fallacies and Narrative Misdirection

A **logical fallacy** is a faulty argument in which something besides reason contributes to the conclusion drawn. Two basic forms of valid reasoning are deduction and induction.

Deductive reasoning moves from a general case to a specific instance of that case. If something is true in general, and an instance is really representative of that general class, then the truth will hold for the specific instance. Syllogisms are examples of deductive reasoning:

Every X is Y.	Something, Y, is true in general of a class called X.
C is X.	C is a member of the class called X.
Therefore, C is Y.	What is true in general of the class called X, is true of each of its members; therefore, Y is true of C.

Fallacies in deductive reasoning come about when the first statement of a syllogism is not true (every X is *not* Y), or if C is assumed to be a member of X when it truly isn't.

Inductive reasoning moves from the particular to the general. It is harder to achieve certainty in this way because you have to determine when you've looked at enough particular examples to be able to draw a general rule that will hold good in all cases. Many fallacies have been named and categorized to make it easier to recognize and remember them. So, for example, here are the three logical fallacies that involve having insufficient evidence to draw valid inductive conclusions.

Hasty generalization—identifying relationships properly, but then drawing a conclusion with too little evidence

Fallacy of exclusion—purposely leaving out evidence that would change the outcome of an inductive argument

Oversimplification—making a complex issue simple by ignoring some of its aspects

How is this important in the Hunger Games Trilogy? Katniss, through whose eyes we experience the story, is a young girl who has been feeding her family since she was 11, who is in her second fight to the death in slightly over a year, and whose education has centered on coal production to the exclusion of much else. In certain ways, her understanding is beyond her years. But she's also in a situation in which she has to make multiple life-and-death decisions without the luxury of time to collect further information or engage in a detailed analysis. So it would be surprising if all of her reasoning were perfect. Besides that, her mistakes contribute to characterization: she's been shown to be a very poor judge of people.

But there's another layer because in this book, the author is using the first-person narrator to shape readers' views of everything that happens. That is, Katniss's errors of logic in addition to revealing character also have a narrative function, acting to shape readers' conclusions and expectations and maintaining suspense by preventing readers from figuring out too much more than Katniss can.

And there's yet another layer—while Katniss is drawing her incorrect conclusions, within Katniss's voice, at times Collins manages to leave us

Directions:
First, read the information. Then, answer the question or questions.

Strategy 19, cont.

clues that Katniss is wrong. In fact, some of these clues are so overt, that a reader may wonder how Katniss could ever have come to the conclusions she did, but that's a criticism of how Collins handles the technique in particular instances, not the technique itself.

One result of these techniques is to create irony, which we discussed in the teaching guide for *The Hunger Games*. To refresh your memory, here is a short recap.

- **Verbal irony** is irony in the use of language. Verbal irony means that what is said is different from, or the opposite of, what is meant.
- In **dramatic irony**, there is knowledge that the narrator makes available to the reader, but the characters are unaware of it. With a first-person narrator, this is a special case because in order to do this, the author must have the narrator tell the audience about things that the narrator him- or herself doesn't understand in such a way that the audience *can* understand—but may not, if they miss the clues.
- **Situational irony** can occur either from the point of view of a character or the reader. It refers to either a) a situation when something that is expected with a great deal of certainty doesn't happen as expected (this can be from either point of view) or b) a situation when something that is intended fails to materialize (this is usually only possible from a character's point of view, except in situations in which the audience participates by making a choice).

When the audience misses hints that disclose dramatic irony, the audience may experience situational irony, because their expectations, like the characters', aren't met.

1. For each example of Katniss's faulty reasoning below, identify
   1) which logical fallacy or fallacies she has fallen prey to,
   2) what the truth of the situation is,
   3) what hints in the text suggest that Katniss is wrong,
   4) what effects this has on the reader's understanding and expectations, and
   5) what kind of irony this created for you and why.

   Example 1: Katniss's interpretation of her interaction with Plutarch Heavensbee at the President's party in Chapter 6.
   Example 2: Katniss's interpretation of events in Chapter 26

2. Compare Collins's treatment of the character of either Johanna Mason or Plutarch Heavensbee to the treatment of any character in another story who seems to be on one side of a good/evil split, but is actually on the other side, for example, any mystery that is presented as a puzzle (that is, the perpetrator is unknown and must be discovered by the protagonist).

Strategy 20

Identifying Themes in a Series

As we discussed in the teaching guide for *The Hunger Games*, the **theme** of a story might be thought of as the story's point or its message. A theme is often a generalization about life or human behavior or values—true, but not a truism—an author's insight into the way things work that he or she wants to share with readers. Through its theme(s), a story moves from the particular (a girl named Katniss; a group of victors forced to fight each other) to the universal.

The message of a story is shaped by the author's intention and purpose. Besides patterns in the story (which often point to the theme), there are certain parts of a story that often refer to the theme: the title, the beginning, and the very end. An important character's first and final words are also likely to carry powerful indications of theme. In a story, such as the Hunger Games trilogy, that deals with complex issues, there are likely to be multiple themes. But also try looking for a joining of the plots with a single, over-arching theme.

How is theme different in a series than in a stand-alone book? In a series, authors, obviously, have more room to develop themes. But in addition to additional space, themes that repeat across individual books or are further developed in subsequent books may gain additional depth and weight.

1. Explain how *Catching Fire* repeats, extrapolates, or displaces the themes of *The Hunger Games*.

Directions: First, read the information. Then, answer the question or questions.

Writer's Forum 7

Comparing Two Treatments

When a book series has been adapted as movies, it is natural to compare the book version and the movie version of the same part of the story, as well as comparing the success of each vehicle overall. To do either of these tasks thoroughly, you need to employ both evaluation techniques and comparison and contrast techniques. Of course, multiple readings/viewings will make it easier to conduct your assessment.

Evaluation involves holding up something to a set of preestablished criteria and then judging it based on those criteria. In comparing two editions that both tell the same story, you would evaluate the main elements of a narrative—like style, dialogue, characterization, plot, setting, themes, and generic expectations (expectations about the genre, such as that fairy tales will begin with "Once upon a time")—as well as assess how well each carries out its part in the overall plot structure. Stepping outside the story, you should also consider consistency. Is the book or movie version internally consistent (in each title and/or overall)? Is the adaption consistent with the original, and if not, are changes made for what appear to be good reasons, and do they work?

Finally, you would compare and contrast the two editions, based on your evaluations, as well as assessing how each makes meaning and achieves its effects within the capacities and limitations of the medium used.

Here are some other questions that would be useful to examine, citing evidence as appropriate:

- A movie is often around two hours long, so a movie adaptation of a book generally leaves out material included in the book. What, if anything, is omitted or compressed in the movie(s)? How did this affect the telling?
- A movie script may have additional material not included in the book, or may make changes in the book. What additions and/or changes do you notice? Did they add value?
- How did your imaginings of the characters, settings, and actions of the book differ from the way they were presented in the movie? Compare the characterizations and the plots carefully. Did the movie provide you with new insights into the plot or characters?
- Apart from the book, did the movie work as an experience in itself? Did it hold your interest? Was it worthwhile? Is it consistent with the first movie in the trilogy?
- Did the theme(s) you identified in the book come out in the movie? If not, what message(s) did the movie give?
- Which did you like better—the book or the movie? Why?

1. Write an essay comparing and contrasting the book and movie versions of *Catching Fire* (2013).
2. Write a first draft of an essay comparing and contrasting *The Hunger Games* trilogy in book and movie form based on the first two titles of each. You will complete this assignment in the next teaching guide, *Mockingjay: A Teaching Guide*.

Directions: First, read the information. Then, answer the question or questions.

Test: Chapters 19–27

Vocabulary

Look at each group of words. Tell why it is important in the story.

1. tar, glob, ghastly, decomposing, slather
2. centrifugal, deceleration, waterlogged
3. double-deal, locket, time-out
4. slack, snags, festooned.
5. flipper, semiconscious, motor coordination

Essay Topics

1. Trace the history of interdistrict connections formed thus far in the trilogy despite the separation strategies imposed by the Capitol.

2. When her prep team arrives before the Victory Tour, Katniss comments on the lives of Capitol citizens. But she then questions what her personality and conversation would be like had she been raised in the Capitol (p. 38). Based on this statement and other evidence from *The Hunger Games* and *Catching Fire* consider Collins's take on the nature/nurture question: are people in Panem entirely shaped by their upbringing? If not, what other forces contribute to their personalities?

3. How did your understanding of Haymitch's promise to Katniss in Chapter 13 change as you read *Catching Fire*?

4. Katniss scoffs when Peeta says, "You're the healer" in Chapter 21. What do you think he meant? Why do you think Collins included this detail? Explain.

5. How are the requirements of being the mockingjay at odds with what Katniss wants for herself?

6. Compare the end of *Catching Fire* to the end of *The Giver* or *Lord of the Flies*.

7. On page 389, Katniss calls Peeta "a good liar." In what instances can we be sure that Peeta has lied? Site evidence to support your conclusions.

8. Explain the meaning of the title *Catching Fire*.

9. What does it mean that Katniss is the mockingjay? Does Katniss's role as the mockingjay justify Haymitch's deception? Explain why you think as you do.

10. If Katniss had been in on the plan, what do you think would have happened? Provide evidence to support your conjectures. Does this justify deceiving her?

11. If the rebellion is to succeed, what changes need to take place in the current state of things?

12. Assess the use of the parachutes in *Catching Fire* in terms of narrative function.

13. Looking at *Catching Fire* as the second act of the trilogy, identify the second reversal or plot point.

Theme Pages

Odds and Chance

1. *The odds,* and whether or not they are in one's favor, is a recurrent consideration in this book. Analyze the effect of the person who chooses names of children for reaping saying to them, "May the odds be ever in your favor?"

2. How are the odds important (or not) in what happens to Katniss? To Panem overall? Explain other factors that contribute to how and why things happen in Panem.

Debts and Owing

1. *Owing* others and how this affects relationships and choices is another repeated consideration in the trilogy. What is Katniss's response to owing others?

2. Consider why owing is so important to Katniss. To understand her situation better, list all the situations and actions that lead Katniss to feel like she is in another person's debt. How would you categorize them?

3 Which character(s) in the trilogy so far have been most comfortable with expressing gratitude? Why do you think this is?

4. According to Italian historian and philosopher Niccolò Machiavelli, the Roman historian Tacitus wrote that "Men are more ready to repay an injury than a benefit because gratitude is a burden and revenge a pleasure." Analyze this observation in the light of the trilogy.

Appearance vs. Reality

1. Appearance can be different from reality for many reasons. List as many reasons as you can for a gap between how someone seems and who he or she really is.

2. Backstory is further details about characters, including how and why they became the way they are. Backstory can help provide depth to a character that seems to be a stereotype. For which characters in *Catching Fire* did additional information from their backstory change and deepen your impression of them? Explain what happened in each case.

3. Machiavelli wrote in his Discourses that "the great majority of mankind are satisfied with appearances, as though they were realities, and are often even more influenced by the things that seem than by those that are." To whom in Panem can this quotation be most clearly applied? Explain.

4. All the allies outside of District 12 were asked to carry out a deception. Evaluate their success.

5. How does Cinna deceive Katniss in *Catching Fire*? Why isn't this dealt with, do you think?

Competition, Alliance, and Self-Interest

1. Competition—especially competition to the death—is inherently at odds with alliance. Based on the first two books of the trilogy, what personal qualities can make alliances possible even in such situa-

Theme Pages

tions? What various actions do competitors in the trilogy take to forge alliances?

2. Think of situations in normal life in which competition and alliance are combined. How are they made to work together?

3. The Greek historian Thucydides wrote that "the only sure basis of an alliance is for each party to be equally afraid of the other." Analyze this thought in the context of Katniss and Finnick.

4 Writer and activist Frances Moore Lappé wrote that "Furthering the common good does not require that we forego self-interest, but rather that we are able to see our own interests linked to those of others." Philosopher and political economist Adam Smith wrote that "By pursuing his own interest [an individual] frequently promotes that of the society more effectually than when he really intends to promote it." Analyze these two quotations in terms of Panem.

Abuse

1. What different kinds of *abuse* are there in the world? Which types play a role in the Hunger Games trilogy?

2. Both Haymitch and Katniss abuse alcohol in *Catching Fire*. Why does each of them turn to alcohol? Given the resources actually available to them, what, if any, alternative could you suggest to deal with the issues that made alcohol attractive to them? Explain.

3. Haymitch stops drinking to train. What leads him to start again?

4. All citizens of Panem, but especially the children, are abused. Who is responsible for the abuse of children? Who is culpable? What's the difference? Use the Choice Tool in your explanation.

Morality and Virtue

1. Morality is a system of behavior standards or a code of right conduct. There is no code of right behavior in Panem that we know of. Though the word *virtue* can be used as a synonym for morality, it can also refer to highly-regarded qualities or traits. In this second sense, virtue can exist without reference to a moral code, but virtues are often considered to be characteristics that make a better individual and society. What virtues do you find in Panem?

2. Katniss finds herself in a dilemma over killing Finnick. Explain her predicament in terms of virtue.

3. In his Farewell Address, George Washington wrote, "Reason and experience both forbid us to expect that national morality can prevail in exclusion of religious principle." Assess this analysis in terms of Panem.

Answer Pages

Strategy 1, Beginning the Second Book in a Series, page 11

1. Genre: science fiction or speculative fiction; Narrator: Katniss Everdeen; Protagonist(s): Katniss, but also arguably Peeta, Rue, the districts; Antagonist(s): the Capitol, President Snow; Inciting Incident: Prim being reaped; Reversal: President Snow's plans to take revenge on Katniss for her trick with the berries.
2. Possible response: the book will be about President Snow's attempts to take revenge on Katniss.
3. Possible response: The title links to Katniss as the "girl on fire"; her fiery spirit of resistance will spread.
4. Possible response: Only "Spark" has a clear connection to the book title, and suggests the beginning of something. [President Snow's reference (p. 23) to Katniss providing a spark that could destroy Panem clarifies the meaning.] *Quell* means "to put an end to [a rebellion] by force," and *the enemy* would seem to mean President Snow, so maybe President Snow will try to quell the spark and then have a face-off with Katniss. In considering possible parallels to *HG*, students may infer that the tributes somehow provide a spark; that *quell* is somehow equivalent to "The Games"; and that—if the victor of the Hunger Games is considered to be President Snow—the enemy is the equivalent of the victor.
5. The reference to the odds not being in Katniss's favor; who Effie Trinket is, and what her presence indicates; what the prep team will do to "beautify" Katniss; why Katniss would want to forget the Hunger Games; which children Katniss killed; what the woods mean to Katniss; the background of Katniss's relationship with Gale and their hunting partnership.
6. Answers will vary. Possible response: The growing connections between districts may spark a revolution that President Snow attempts to quell, leading to a confrontation between Katniss and President Snow.

PART I THE SPARK—Chapter 1, Back in District 12, pages 12–13

1. Possible response: Katniss's travel plans suggest that her influence will broaden; President Snow's presence in District 12 suggests that he continues to view Katniss as a threat and will act to contain her.
2. Students should recognize the change in tone and purpose. In *HG*, Katniss used the phrase in a joking way, with irony. In *CF*, she has adopted it as a way to analyze her world, showing that she has internalized the thinking involved in the "advertising" of the Games.
3. She would like to forget the Games and pretend they never happened. The requirement that she participate in the Victory Tour prevents her from acting on her preference.
4. As a winner, Katniss is wealthy enough for her family to buy meat from the butcher, so she no longer hunts from necessity (to stay alive) as she used to, but mainly to help support Gale's family..
5. He is expert at luring animals into imaginatively created traps. Possible responses: he will use his hunting skills on the forces from the Capitol; he will help make it possible for a large group of people to escape the system of districts and stay alive in the woods.
6. Katniss's lament that she can't forget the Games; her sadness about her changed elationship with Gale; her preference for her old home; the poor fit of her new clothes in contrast to the comfort of her old ones.
7. Answers should include: what she purchases, her attitude about shopping, the fact that she now arrives with money to make purchases but nothing to trade.
8. Her exchange with Cray is friendly, but not intimate: if she trusted him, she wouldn't have lied for Haymitch; if he were hostile, he wouldn't have accepted her lie so easily. Darius teases her like a brother.
9. Possible response: Perhaps things between her and Peeta have become awkward now that they're home, so she's reluctant to accept (or buy) bread from him.
10. Given the popular romance between Katniss and Peeta, Gale didn't fit the story, so a news reporter decided—based on their similar appearance (gray eyes, dark hair, olive skin)—to portray Gale as Katniss's cousin instead, and the residents of District 12 let it go.
11. Haymitch's house shows that his misery doesn't lift with the passing of a particular edition of the Hunger Games. He doesn't care for himself or his home, and his arena experience leads him to sleep with a knife.
12. They are polite, but formal and stiff, distant and uncomfortable.
13. Students should grasp that Miss America spends a year on tour in her role as advocate for the platform she has chosen to espouse, speaking to a targeted audience to effect social change. Victors of the Hunger Games tour the Capitol and the districts whose tributes they may have killed personally so that the Capitol can remind the districts of its power over them and Capitol citizens of the entertainments it provides.
14. Her mother's odd laugh, holding Katniss's arm "as if to stop" her, pale face, implicit lie about where Katniss has been, and anxious voice; the presence of the man whose suit and features show he's from the Capitol.
15. Answers will vary. Students may suggest that he wears a rose as a boutonnière to cover-up the smell of blood, which could come from some unhealed wound or from the fact that he's a vampire.
16. Answers should include only include elements/situations that Mrs. Everdeen experienced.

Strategy 2, Understanding the Series Reading Process, pages 14–15

1. Information is spread throughout the chapter in Katniss's and other's words. Name: Darius calls her "Miss Everdeen" p. 11; her mother calls her "Katniss" p. 16; Family members: "my mother and my little sister Prim" p. 4, "father . . . killed in an explosion" p. 5; Location: "the woods" p. 3, "District 12" p. 5, "my old home" p. 6, "Gale's house" p. 7, "the Hob" p. 9, "Victor's Village" p. 12, "Haymitch's house" p. 13, "my house" p. 16, "the study" p. 17; Appearance: "fine wool coat," "expensive machine-made shoes" p. 6, "braid" p. 11, "dark straight hair, olive skin, gray eyes" p. 12

2. In their first encounter, Katniss tried to drown Buttercup. By the reaping in *HG*, Katniss was sharing entrails from her hunting kills and Buttercup had stopped hissing at her. By the start of the Victory Tour, Katniss has discovered that she and the cat both prefer their old house in the Seam, rather than the house in the Victor's Village; she now feeds him parts of her catch that could be food (i.e., not just entrails), and spends time petting him. Without the background, the growth in their relationship would not be evident.

3. The reader who missed the reference in the sentence would not realize that what Katniss made fun of in *The Hunger Games* has now become a measure of her interactions in *Catching Fire*, showing one effect that participating in the Games has had on her.

4. The last two paragraphs are about Katniss losing her deep connection to Peeta on account of the forced romance during the Games. The words "slipping away from me" could lead to an expectation that the distance would increase. The words "dreading the moment when I will finally have to let go" could lead to the expectation that Katniss would fight to keep the relationship. In either case, readers probably didn't expect that it would be p. 9 before Peeta is even mentioned. Without this expectation, readers would not be as surprised by the distance and might miss the significance of Katniss buying buns at the Hob.

5. Possibile responses: Curiosity about Katniss's romantic life, now that she is somewhat estranged from both Gale and Peeta; further conflict with President Snow; high emotions on the Victory Tour—particularly in districts whose tributes were killed by Katniss or Peeta—and a lot of pain in District 11.

Strategy 3, Charting Character Development, page 16

1. Key events for each age range: <11 Father teaches Katniss to hunt; 11 Father dies in mine explosion, Peeta throws her bread; she starts hunting and gathering to feed her family, taking over running the household from her seriously depressed mother; 12–15 She signs up for tesserae, meets Gale and becomes his hunting partner and best friend; 16 *HG* Prim is reaped for the Seventy-Fourth Hunger Games, and Katniss takes her place; costumed by Cinna, Katniss becomes known as "the girl on fire," and—with Haymitch's help and sponsorship from District 12, as well as her own ingenuity and talent, and her threat to commit suicide and leave the Games without a victor—wins the Games, saving Peeta, but incurring President Snow's wrath. 16 *CF* President Snow comes to District 12 and threatens to kill Gale and more if Katniss doesn't do a sufficiently good job of presenting herself as in love with Peeta on the Victory Tour and quell the incipient uprisings in the districts. Learning that President Snow, is not satisfied, she returns to District 12, where—with the help of Haymitch and Peeta—she saves Gale from being whipped to death by Romulus Thread, and meets Bonnie and Twill who recognize her, show her their mockingjay cracker, and tell her District 13 still exists. Caught in the woods when the electrified fence is turned on, Katniss leaps from a branch, reentering the district. She manages to fool the two peacekeepers waiting at her house, hoping she will fail to show up. A few months later, Katniss learns that she will be reaped for the Quarter Quell. She makes Haymitch promise they'll save Peeta. Peeta forces them to train like Careers. In the arena, an alliance masterminded by Haymitch and unknown to Katniss and Peeta forms, including Districts 3, 4, 6, 7, 8, and 11. Beetee is charged with blowing up the force field enclosing the arena, which Katniss ends up doing. Katniss, Finnick, and Beetee are rescued by Plutarch Heavensbee and Haymitch in a hovercraft from District 13, but Peeta, Johanna, and Enobaria are taken alive by the Capitol. Katniss becomes mentally unstable, and nothing reaches her until Gale turns up. He tells her that District 12 has been destroyed, though her mother and Prim are safe.

2. **Prim**: At first, Katniss is the capable one who helps feed Prim and saves her by replacing her when she is reaped; but by *CF*, Prim has both matured and evolved as a healer, helping treat Gale after the whipping and comforting Katniss after the Quarter Quell card is read. **Gale** is initially a hunting partner, then best friend, then romantic interest, confessing in *CF* that he loves Katniss, following which she realizes that she loves him, too, but is not sure how. She gives him up as she heads to the Quarter Quell, determined to continue the staged romance with Peeta and save Peeta's life, but when she is rescued and Peeta is caught, Gale is the only person who can reach her. **Peeta** goes from loving Katniss from afar to risking a beating to give her bread to confessing his love on public television to boost her chance of winning the Games to

realizing that her interest in him was a strategy. After a post-Games hiatus in which they barely speak, he suggests they be friends, and Katniss agrees. They independently plan to sacrifice their lives for each other in the Quell. Thinking they've both been captured, Katniss plans to kill Peeta to spare him from torture and captivity. Discovering she has been rescued and he has been captured, and she says she hates him. **Haymitch**: Before the reaping in *HG*, Katniss knows Haymitch only as a drunk victor. After being in the Games herself and seeing the recap of the Quarter Quell that Haymitch won, her respect for his abilities and her understanding of his alcohol abuse increases. She earns his respect early on in *HG*, but not his trust, and with the goal of keeping her alive and fomenting revolution, he keeps Katniss and Peeta in the dark and manipulates them for the cause in *CF*. Katniss had come to trust him and feels deeply betrayed when she learns of his choices at the end of *CF*. **District 12**: Katniss first related to District 12 (and particularly the Hob) through her father, and when he dies, she seems doomed to the typical end of starving people in the Seam until Peeta, a town boy, provides her with bread—her first strong connection outside her region. When she starts to hunt, she begins to relate to the traders in the Hob, and town's folk—like the baker, the mayor, and even Peacekeepers—in her own right as a hunter. The silence at the reaping when Effie asks for applause and the salute that she receives when she takes Prim's place show a united District 12. It isn't until *CF* that she finds out that both the Hob and the wider District 12 sponsored her in the Games, helping save her life. In *CF,* she becomes something of a patron, spreading her winnings around the Hob to benefit a wide group of sellers. **Other Districts**: The Capitol has measures in place to keep the districts separate, and this keeps Katniss from knowing much about the other districts until the Games. She has held Capitol residents in derision, but her stereotypes are challenged when she meets Cinna. She begins to learn about work in other districts as she trains and in the Games. She allies with Rue from District 11, and both Katniss giving Rue the District 12 salute and receiving a gift of bread from District 11 after Rue dies are notable firsts in interdistrict relations. Thresh then spares her life because of her alliance with Rue. On the Victory Tour in *CF*, though she fears facing the communities whose children she has killed (or who died in the course of her victory), Peeta's gift and her speech, as well as her meaning as the mockingjay, earn her a salute from District 11 and make her a growing sign of hope to rebels across Panem, as shown by the mockingjay on Bonnie and Twill's cracker and—though Katniss does not understand it—on Plutarch Heavensbee's watch. The victors had already bonded, but Katniss's personal power is so great that it is the focal point for alliances that last through the Quarter Quell, leading to the rescue / attempted rescue of all the remaining tributes.

3. Katniss's familial relationships are moving towards relationships of equals, rather than being one-sided with Katniss as the caregiver. Her relationship with Peeta first moves towards more balance (when they choose friendship), but because of President Snow's mandate and their both being reaped for the Quarter Quell, is thrown out of balance again. By Chapter 27, she says she hates him. Because of the Quarter Quell, Katniss's relationship with Gale, which has been more passionate and explosive, is severed completely, and when it is continued, has an unnatural dynamic because Katniss is mentally ill and Gale has to tell her such devastating news. Katniss's relationship with Haymitch starts off unequal because he is her mentor, and then becomes more of equals after the games when, for example, as she feels able to throw cold water on him to wake him without fear of repercussions, but is marred by the fact that he becomes her mentor again and he is using her to serve the revolution without telling her. Katniss's relationships within her own district and other districts have gone from nothing to powerful—first connecting her to other socioeconomic/status groups within her district, then, starting with Rue, to District 11 as a whole and other districts who saw her "trick with the berries" as defiance of the Capitol.

Chapter 2, A Visit from the President, pages 18–19

1. In *HG* (p. 175), Katniss says that in trying to evade the fireballs, she might fall into a pit of vipers, but she can't worry about that possibility. Following that same approach, when Katniss uses the berries to keep herself and Peeta alive, she doesn't consider the consequences outside the immediate, desperate situation. However, her "trick with the berries" incurs President Snow's animosity, bringing the "viper" to her house.
2. In *CF* (p. 18), Katniss says that the berries were intended to keep herself and Peeta alive and "any act of rebellion was purely coincidental." But then she adds, "But when the Capitol decrees that only one tribute can live and you have the audacity to challenge it, I guess that's a rebellion in itself." On p. 20, she says, "That was the moment when I guessed that if the Gamemakers had to choose between watching Peeta and me commit suicide—which would mean having no victor—and letting us both live, they would take the latter." There are clear differences: First, she claims a focus on life for herself and Peeta, whereas her added comment (p. 18) redefines it as a revolutionary act, and on p. 20, her motivation is, again, life, with a focus on the means of achieving her goal (coercing the Gamemakers) Students may point out that none of this

matches the more complex analysis (*HG* p. 358). [See Chapter 8 for further analysis of motivation.]

3. Possible response: To trick/lure Katniss into telling the truth and believing that he will do so, too.
4. Capitol citizens would have been furious and the districts would all have a shared experience of the Capitol killing their children, possibly leading to more solidarity between and among districts and outrage at the Capitol for not even allowing one of the 24 tributes to live, fomenting unrest. Snow wants to both scare her by showing what happens to people who cross him and make her feel responsible for district unrest.
5. Because many products in Panem both come from a single district and are made only for Capitol consumption, and with the producers having no control over pricing, the control left within their power is ceasing production, which would create shortages only for the Capitol. This is a fragility of the (otherwise very tightly controlled) system that President Snow may have been referring to. [Students will not know until later that he may also have been referring to fragility resulting from having allowed District 13 to survive.]
6. On p. 22, Katniss says she's surprised by the "directness and even the sincerity of this speech" and in the next sentence suggests that the speech is insincere, so it is not an accurate assessment. The cleanest explanation is that the word *apparent* should appear before *sincerity* and somehow got dropped.
7. Possible responses: I would if believed that she were so gullible that she would unquestioningly believe that uprisings would be a terrible thing and her fault, and could make her so focused on behaving herself that she wouldn't stir up unrest in the districts or foster interdistrict unity on the Victory Tour. Presenting Katniss with the idea that she could foster a revolution is short-sighted and foolish, especially when Seneca Crane's decision to let her live shows that she has (unwitting) influence within Snow's inner circle.
8. The kiss with Gale took place by the hole under the fence nearest the Hob, so could have been seen by a spy in the vicinity, but in the woods, cameras and microphones would have been needed.
9. Even though Katniss does not explicitly contrast them, readers may be led to do so..
10. Possible response: Katniss acting in love with Peeta cannot possibly distract restive residents plotting uprisings or rebellion, but it may keep her focused and limit the damage she causes on the Victory Tour.
11. Answers should include: he comes into her home and takes control; he makes her wait while he continues to read; he threatens her indirectly (by alluding to Seneca Crane's death), by revealing that he knows things that she thought were private (her meetings with Gale, that he's not her cousin, that Gale kissed her), and explicitly threatens Gale, and tells her that the tour is her only chance to satisfy him.

Strategy 4, Plot—Analyzing the Use of Flashback, Recap, and Foreshadowing, page 19

1. New information includes: Gale, whose last name is *Hawthorne*, works in the coal mines, limiting hunting time; Katniss's and Gale's relationship has changed; more about Gale's skill with snares. Combining recap with new information keeps the reader who knows all the recap information engaged with the story.
2. Sample responses: **Foreshadowing:** p. 3 passage beginning "By noon they will all be." **Flashback:** p. 12 passage beginning "When Peeta and I"; pp. 25–28 passage beginning "After Peeta and I got home from the Games." **Recap:** p. 4 sentence starting "Back when we were in school"; p. 5 passage beginning "Every year in school"; p. 9 passage beginning "Before my fellow tribute." These all contribute to understanding Katniss's current situation, mental state, and choices, as foundation for the rest of the book.

Strategy 5, Analyzing Choices, pages 20–21

Choice	Type	Motivation	Information	Extent
Katniss's choice of how to behave on the tour	terrorized choice	Avoiding harm to her family, p. 18; avoiding her own death, pp. 19–20; avoiding contributing to an uprising that would (according to President Snow) cause many deaths, terrible conditions, and the collapse of "the entire system," p. 21; avoiding President Snow killing Gale and Peeta p. 28	Partial information, some of which is false, due to lies and/or invalid conclusions (about the results of an uprising); Katniss is not aware of the level of information.	Final—"This tour will be your only chance to turn things around" p. 29

Strategy 6, Analyzing Control of the Setting, page 22

Chapter	Instance of Control	Who Controls?	Chapter	Instance of Control	Who Controls?
1	Katniss activities in woods	Katniss	1	Katniss visiting Hazelle, the Hob	Katniss
1	Where Katniss and family live	Capitol	1–2	Katniss's study	President Snow
3	Katniss's bathroom	Prep team	3	Katniss's living room	Cinna
3	Katniss's front doorway	Effie Trinket	3	Train inside vs. outside	Haymitch

Writer's Forum 1, Translating Fiction Into Drama, page 23

1. Students' scenes will vary. Scenes should combine stage directions and dialogue in an appropriate format. The choices made to transform narration into drama should be defensible.

Chapter 3, The Victory Tour Begins, page 24

1. Possible response: Issues in Panem run so deep and the government treats citizens so poorly that nothing Katniss can do can possibly quell the uprising, but her focus on demonstrating her love for Peeta may prevent her charisma and growing celebrity status from bonding the districts together. [Some students may only realize this in the course of the narration of the tour or afterwards.]
2. Katniss has bcome less resentful and angry with her mother and believes she must protect her, although her mother shows signs of increasing strength and ability to protect Katniss. Katniss finds a parallel between her mother's depression after the death of Mr. Everdeen and her own current situation. Seeing her stylists respond to her mother, she wonders what she would have been like if she had been born in the Capitol, implicitly questioning how much they were shaped by their upbringing and environment.
3. Like the speaker in the poem Katniss measures her change against the unchanging backdrop of nature. She says, "The lake's remarkably unchanged, and I'm almost unrecognizable" (p. 34). The speaker in the poem observes that "all's changed" in his life since he first watched and counted the swans, 19 years before.
4. The Capitol will not release its grip on Katniss after the Victory Tour: Katniss must go on being in love with Peeta forever to satisfy it.
5. Students summaries should be limited to what Mrs. Everdeen saw/experienced.

Strategy 7, Challenging the Status Quo, pages 25–26

1. We have the right to 1) peacably assemble—to get together in groups for whatever activities or dicussions we choose, as long as they're not illegal; 2) freedom of speech, which allows us to comment on, and even crticize, the government; 3) petition the government to put grievances to rights; 4) keep and bear arms; 5) be secure in our persons, houses, papers, and effect against unreasonable searches and seizures, and warrants that allow search and seizure are only to be issued when there is probable cause; 6) a speedy and public trial by an impartial jury of our peers when we are accused of crimes. Students may conclude that lack of rights is likely to make citizens resentful and distrustful of the government of Panem, and lead them to have to take extraordinary measures (uprisings, terrorism, revolution) to pursue a change of government.
2. Students may agree that citizens of Panem face just such a situation,with no means to address issues within the system, but they may point out that the definition fails to address terrorism *by* a government.

Chapter 4, Choosing Friendship; Arrival in District 11, pages 27–28

1.

Choice	Type	Motivation	Information	Extent
Katniss's romantic future is limited to marriage with Peeta and no other options	terrorized choice	Saving her own life, the lives of her family and friends, and preventing death and destruction that President Snow saw would follow uprisings.	Partial information mixed with lies from both Haymitch—who is planning a revolution [students will not know this at this point in the story]—and President Snow; partial awareness	Seems final—turns out not to be after revolution, when she does get to choose [Students will not know this at this point in the story.]
District 12 inhabitants' romantic partners are likely limited to District 12	Apparently free (including across social boundaries, like the Everdeens, and staying single, like Haymitch)	Happiness; possibly life needs	Dependent on individual circumstances	Divorce and separation aren't mentioned, so decisions seem final

Students answers for themselves will vary depending on their culture and family. Some students may be free; others may come from cultures with arranged marriages. Some may bring up the rights of gays to marry (or not) where they live.

2. She comes to understand that he might have chosen his current state because he shares her fear of having a child go into the arena (it seems that reapings are rigged to 'favor' victors' children).
3. Possible responses: It made them look younger, making their deaths more poignant and distressing; it pre-

vented the appearance of a very unfair fight between contestants who look like grown men and those who look like children.

4. Answers will vary. Perhaps she would have tried telling President Snow that Peeta just wanted to be friends; perhaps she would have consulted Peeta about staging the most convincing romantic act.
5. Students may surmise that the Capitol would not approve of Peeta's, partly because it shows cross-district sympathy, portraying all tributes as victims (rather than, say, glorifying District 12's victors). Others might think that they will approve because it helps keep the terror alive. Some students may find it strange after reading Chapter 17 that no reaction from the Capitol is recorded, when—in contrast—such a big deal is made about Peeta's painting performance for the Gamemakers, and consider it a continuity lapse.
6. Open fields vs. heavy woods; the height, deadliness, and construction of the electrified fence; the watchtowers with armed guards; poorer housing; the size and population of the district. Possible response: the portability and consumability food make theft a greater risk in District 11 than District 12.
7. Peacekeepers want to limit the audience size, given Katniss's popularity, or be in a locale they feel they can control. Perhaps Collins aimed to show the irony of the actions occurring before the Justice Building.
8. Bringing the families of dead tributes as close as possible to tributes who survived and may even have murdered their children seems likely to bolster antagonism between districts. Due to both existing understanding and empathy between Katniss and District 11 from the Games and also to Peeta's and Katniss's gestures in their speeches, instead of increased antipathy, there is increased fellow-feeling and respect.
9. Students many feel that the growing unrest and the view of Katniss as a symbol of defying the Capitol are already too deeply rooted to be defused by anything she could possibly say (or do).
10. Rue's reproachful sister would only know what happened starting on p. 58 when Effie pushes the victors out the door through to the shooting of the old man, with the exception of Katniss's thoughts.

Strategy 8, Predicting and Recognizing Others' Perceptions, page 29

1. Haymitch, Cinna, Peeta, and Caesar most readily predict and recognize others' points of view, and, Finnick is astute in his treatment of Katniss in the arena.
2. Possible responses: Thread knows Katniss is breaking the law, and despises her for interfering in his punishment of Gale and hopes to catch her outside the district so he can 'legitimately' punish or kill her. Johanna first thinks Katniss is a prude, then a pain for demanding the rescue of Beetee and Wiress, but agrees to risk her life to save her, and does her part. Beetee and Wiress trust her quickly, telling her about the "chink in the armor." Wiress is pleased when the clock is understood, and Beetee doesn't expose her lie about her ear. Both risk their lives for her. Finnick teases her with seduction and trusts and helps her and Peeta, but recognizes that she doesn't completely trust him, although he risks his life for them.
3. Answers will vary depending on which characters students wrote about in question 2.

Writer's Forum 2, Comparing/Contrasting Books in a Series, page 30

1. Students' should use one of the two comparison–contrast structures and include the following: **a.** In *HG*, Katniss is anticipating the reaping, along with Gale, who shares her ironic view of the Capitol. In *CF*, Katniss is anticipating the Victory Tour alone, separated from Gale both by his need to work and the coolness between them after the Games and her "romance" with Peeta. **b.** In *HG*, Katniss chooses to offer herself as a volunteer to save her sister, Prim. In *CF*, having won the games and supposedly safe at home, she finds President Snow in her house to threaten her, her family and her friends if she does not convincingly show her love for Peeta to quell the restless districts and stop potential uprisings. **c.** In *HG*, Katniss makes a serious error of judgment about Peeta, concluding (erroneously) that he is determined to win the games and is therefore a threat to her, and this leads her to behave dishonestly and deceptively. In *CF*, Katniss and Peeta agree to be friends and this feels more honest to Katniss.

Chapter 5, Peeta Proposes; President Snow Is Not Satisfied, page 31

1. The aging and lack of care of a rich, beautiful building, and its emblems of religion, culture, and times of plenty. Students may think that this is meant to mirror the state of justice in Panem.
2. Because Haymitch and Katniss have lied to him, Peeta has unwittingly endangered people of District 11, himself and Katniss, and the people he cares for in District 12.
3 If they hadn't seen, they would likely have recognized gunfire without knowing who was shot or why, so they probably wouldn't have felt responsible, Haymitch wouldn't have led them away for a debriefing, and the new understanding with Peeta wouldn't have been established. (Students may note that "backfiring" is a weak explanation, given the state of technology in Panem and the very few vehicles mentioned.)
4. Katniss learns that Haymitch had explicitly chosen to save her, rather than Peeta.

Catching Fire: A Teaching Guide

5. Effie further reveals how obtuse she is and unaware of others' feelings and the impact of her words, while Portia shows her sensitivity and kindness, speaking to prevent Effie from being embarrassed.
6. After visiting Districts 8, 4, and 3, Katniss sees fury and a desire for vengeance in the crowds' behavior (p. 71), leading her to realize that there is nothing she could possibly do to change it.
7. By shaking his head, President Snow answers Katniss's silent question letting her know that she failed to convince him sufficiently of her love for Peeta. It means that she, her family, and her friends are doomed, but she takes it to mean that she cannot possibly gain his approval now, so she is free to stop acting and to save herself and those she cares for, if she can. Note that Peeta is not "fully informed" (p. 67) till p. 103.
8. Summaries should show Effie's obtuseness by including only the surface level of events, not their import.

Strategy 9, Analyzing Assumptions, page 33

1. President Snow makes it sound plausible that Katniss can do what he asks, but if students think about a revolution they know something about (say, the American Revolution), and try to imagine a 16-year-old girl stopping it by acting convincingly in love, they will probably get the idea that the task is impossible.
2. Haymitch is probably right, given the current situation. But students may suggest that the country is in crisis, and things could change: Katniss could end up dead (but the fact that we know that the trilogy goes on for another book makes this unlikely), or the uprisings might turn to full-scale rebellion, restoring Katniss's freedom to choose whom she marries, though she might still marry Peeta or not marry at all.
3. The evidence of Peeta's paintings, his speech in District 11, and his offer to the District 11 tribute families suggest that through Chapter 4, he viewed the tour as an opportunity to strengthen interdistrict bonds and understanding. In Chapter 5, he learns that the tour is about behaving so as to safeguard the lives of family and friends in District 12 and citizens in other districts, which he has put at greater risk without knowing it.
4. Katniss assumes that Haymitch's memory or instincts led him to the dome, since—as far as she knows—he has only been in the building once. Students may suggest that another possibility is that he is somehow in touch with people from District 11.

Strategy 10, Identifying Figures of Speech, page 34

1. Metaphors: p. 63 " . . . a wall of white Peacekeeper uniforms blocks our view" describes being blocked from the murder of the whistler; p. 67–8: "Here in 11, . . . [a] spark could be enough to set them ablaze" describes the mood in District 11; p. 79: "Some crowds have the weary-cattle feel . . . " describe the citizens' mood; p. 73: " . . . we bubble our way through a list of questions" describe a tone they affected; Personification: p. 67 "The dust . . . looks for new places to land" describes the lack of care and housekeeping in the dome.
2. Possible reasons for Katniss's increased use of figures of speech in *CF* vs. *HG* could include greater contact with people from different backgrounds, like Cinna and Haymitch, could be intended to show a change in her character, or could result from an inadvertent stylistic change on Collins' part. There does not seem to be any clear indication in the text about what the use of figurative speech is meant to represent. Given Collins's inexplicable use of very occasional literary references and alliteration in *HG*, it seems possible that she did not make this change intentionally, or that her own style is leaking into Katniss's narration.

Chapter 6, The President's Party; Uprising in District 8, page 35

1. Guy Fawkes, who tried to blow up the Houses of Parliament to wipe out the government of England, is reported to have said these words to James I after his arrest on November 6, 1605. Katniss saying it allies her with the incipient revolution for the reader who recognizes the quotation, even though—given her description of her education in *HG* (p. 41)—it seems unlikely that she knows its source or has ever heard it.
2. Possible response: It suggests the country is 'feeding' on its children, rather than protecting them.
3. He suggests that trying to subdue things in the districts may have been wrong, implying that revolution might be a good thing. He is brought to this conclusion by the prep team's unconscious reminder—by their use of vomiting to be able to eat more—of how barbaric behavior in the Capitol is.
4. Because he is a Gamemaker, Katniss thinks Plutarch is a disgusting human being and doesn't want him touching her. She concludes that his secrecy about his watch is evidence of his vanity at having a unique timepiece that he doesn't want others to copy. Students may conclude—either from Katniss's track record at misinterpreting people and/or because they can read Plutarch better than Katniss can—that he is trying to communicate some message, though there is not enough information to know what the message is.
5. Answers will vary. Some students may expect swift retribution from the Capitol; others may predict a spread of unrest to other districts—though given how cut off the districts are—seemingly each encircled by a more-or-less well-guarded fence—it's unclear just how this might happen.

6. Since Plutarch seems interested in communicating with Katniss, students may believe that he will have been closely observing her, noting her external actions, and even discerning some of her thoughts from her actions. In addition, students may suggest explanations for Plutarch's interactions with Katniss, even predicting that he is giving her a clue about the upcoming games that she will mentor. [Since Plutarch did not know Katniss was going into the arena and since the rescue plan was explicitly concealed from Katniss and Peeta, the disappearance of the mockingjay cannot be interpreted as a hint of the rescue.]

Strategy 11, Understanding How Symbols and Motifs Are Developed, pages 36

1. *HG* p. 38 "Madge . . . leans in and fixes the bird to my dress. 'Promise you'll wear it into the arena, Katniss?'"; pp. 42–3 " . . . something of a slap in the face to the Capitol . . ."; pp. 43–4 "My father was particularly fond of mockingjays . . ."; p. 145 " . . . it's your district token . . ."; pp. 211–2 " . . . That's how I decided I could trust you . . ."; p. 213 " . . . decides to teach me her mockingjay signal . . ."; p. 235 "Then, almost eerily, the mockingjays take up my song . . ."; p. 329 " . . . Then the whole world comes alive with the sound . . ."; p. 370 " . . . nothing to take but the mockingjay pin Madge gave me." *CF* p. 41 "My mother hurries up with something cupped in her hand. . . . Cinna fixes it on the knot in the scarf."; pp. 61–62 " . . . someone whistles Rue's four-note mockingjay tune . . ."; p. 78 "Apparently my mockingjay pin has spawned a new fashion sensation . . ."; pp. 82–3 " . . . It's another mockingjay. Exactly like the pin on my dress. Only this one disappears . . ."; pp. 91–92 "'It was my aunt's,' . . . A mockingjay is a creature the Capitol never intended to exist . . ."; p. 139 "It's my mockingjay. . . . My bird baked into bread . . ."; p. 163 " . . . unmistakeable flash of that same mockingjay's wing . . ."; p. 190 "Effie doesn't know that my mockingjay pin is now a symbol used by the rebels . . ."; pp. 196–7 "Of my mockingjay pin and how it means something completely different now that I know that its former owner was Madge's aunt, Maysilee Doner, a tribute who was murdered in the arena."; pp. 252–4 " . . . Cinna has turned me into a mockingjay . . . I can tell [Caesar] knows that the mockingjay isn't just my token. That it's come to symbolize so much more . . ."; p. 267 "I owe it to Cinna, who risked everything by undermining President Snow and turning my bridal silk into mockingjay plumage. And I owe it to the rebels who, emboldened by Cinna's example, might be fighting to bring down the Capitol at this moment." pp. 282–3 " . . . chain around his neck. My mockingjay has been engraved on it. . . ."; p. 327 "And then my mockingjay lit up briefly and vanished. In retrospect it's like he was giving me a clue . . ."; p. 386–8 "'We had to save you because you're the mockingjay, Katniss . . . While you live, the revolution lives. . .' . . . I'm the mockingjay and it's too hard keeping me alive as it is." Summary sentences should mention the growth of Katniss's understanding of the meaning of the mockingjay pin, as well as the districts' increasing identification of her with mockingjays through the pin, association with Rue and her mockingjay song, and the parallel between Katniss's and the mockingjays' unplanned existence.

2. In *HG*, the symbolic meaning of fire is mostly related to Katniss as the girl on fire. With the title of *CF* and his discussion with Katniss at her home, President Snow shifts the symbolism to Katniss as providing "a spark that, left unattended, may grow" (p. 23)—he says, "to an inferno that destroys Panem," but students may see the possibility that the Capitol could be destroyed without all of Panem being destroyed as well.

3. In addition to *Hawthorne* and *Hazelle*, these names should appear. **Latin:** *Darius* – means "upholder of the good" – a fair and honest Peacekeeper; *Seneca Crane* – Seneca was a roman statesman and dramatist who was forced to commit suicide for allegedly participating in a conspiracy to assassinate the emperor; the manner of his death accords better with the portrayal of his death in the movie of *HG* (2012); *Plutarch Heavensbee* – there's no clear connection for this name with any of the three historical Plutarchs, but the name Plutarch means "source of riches," and as the leader of the revolution, he could be considered the source of all good things that come from it; *Romulus Thread* – Romulus became the sole founder of Rome by slaying his twin brother Remus, appropriate because the Head Peacekeeper is willing to go to any lengths. *Brutus* – more likely connected with the word *brute* than with the politician who co-lead the conspiracy that assassinated Julius Caesar; *Enobaria* – feminine form of *Enobarbus*, altered form of *Ahenobarbus*; most likely referencing Gnaeus Domitius Ahenobarbus, who was captured and then pardoned by Julius Caesar: the relevance becomes clear in *Mockingjay,* when Katniss bargains for her (and others') release. **Nature:** *Cray* – the crayfish or crawdad feeds off animals and plants that are living or dead: a Peacekeeper who abuses citizens in his own district; *Twill* – a type of woven fabric; District 8 provides clothing to the Capitol; *Finnick Odair* – the fin is an important part of a fish's anatomy, and District 4 provides seafood to the Capitol; Odair/Adair means "noble spear," which may connect to his sense of honor in the alliance and abilities w/ the trident, technically a type of spear; *Chaff* – husks of seeds and corn, removed before consumption and *Seeder* – machine for sowing seeds, critical in District 11, both appropriate to an agricultural district; *Annie Cresta* – likely from the crest of a wave, which is related to the seafood-based livelihood of District 4 residents.

Writer's Forum, 3 Writing a Short Research Report, page 37

1. Answers will vary somewhat, depending on sources. When students have handed in their papers, ask if they found information about vomitoriums. When they have told you what they learned, share this online article with them: http://www.straightdope.com/columns/read/2421/were-there-really-vomitoriums-in-ancient-rome It is likely that at least some of your students may have read an article in which the definition was incorrect or referred to a vomitorium in the president's mansion in their report. You may wish to use this opportunity to start a conversation about the problems of finding reliable, authoritative sources. If they used semingly authoritative sources that got this wrong, consider that it may not be appropriate to mark them down for this error, due to its proliferation even in sources that seem to be credible.

Chapter 7, Meeting Gale at the Lake to Plan an Escape, pages 38–39

1. Madge thinks of mockingjays as "just songbirds," while Katniss understands the mockingjay as a creature that the Capitol "never intended to exist," but that survived through its own "will to live." Students may realize that Katniss resembles the mockingjay in these qualities.
2. Given the other evidence of Gale's distaste for Katniss's Capitol connections and refusal to accept any of her winnings, it's likely that he is speaking ironically and expects to hate her plan or find it repulsive.
3. He takes it to mean that she is giving up her winnings from the Games and her new connections for (love of) him.
4. Katniss thinks her response is the "worst" because rather than expressing her feelings for Gale, she says, "I know." Students may agree with her or think she was honest. They may also fault Collins, either because it doesn't make sense for Katniss to say "I never see these things coming" (p. 97) and four sentences later say, "I know" (does she know or not?) or for repeating Han Solo's response when Princess Leia says she loves him in *The Empire Strikes Back*.
5. Answers will vary. Students who don't understand how President Snow has manipulated Katniss may agree with her. Those who have seen through his spiel are more likely to agree with Gale.
6. Summaries should capture Gale's alternating sense of frustration and elation in this chapter, and reflect on how and why he dislikes Katniss's connections with Haymitch, Peeta, and anyone from the Capitol, as well as her winnings from the Games.

Strategy 12, Understanding Complex Motivations, page 40

1. Katniss, who is drawn to Gale, but forced to marry Peeta, whether she wants to or not; Haymitch,who is forced to mentor and choose between tributes in the hopes of being able to save just one of them.
2. Peeta,who wants to marry Katniss and is being forced to do so.
3. Gale, who won't accept any gifts from the Capitol and can barely contain his rage against it; the Whistler of District 11, who dies for his part in District 11's honoring of Katniss.
4. Effie and all members of Katniss's prep team seem to be fairly oblivious tools of the Capitol, doing their jobs, and missing the bigger picture.
5. Katniss says she believes Cinna is at risk (*CF* p. 33), and it's certainly possible to interpret his presentations of Katniss and Peeta (including, for example, the hand-holding in the first chariot ride [*HG*, p. 69] and dressing Katniss to make her look innocent for the post-berry interview) as intentionally not serving the Capitol's interests. Caesar Flickerman takes steps to protect Katniss in her final interview after the Games (*HG*, pp. 366–70), which may be indicative of the motivation described.

Chapter 8, The Whipping, page 41

1. According to Bristel, Darius tried to stop Thread disrespectfully by saying it was enough and grabbing Thread's arm. Haymitch tried intimidation, threatening to inform the Capitol. Katniss cried, "No!" and inserted herself between Thread and Gale. Purnia respectfully suggested that the required punishment had been fulfilled, but left an opening for Thread to override it, calling him "sir," speaking unemotionally, and stepping forward from her place in a line of Peacekeepers without approaching Thread too closely.
2. Collins sometimes uses it to provide recap and help shape the reader's anticipation (p. 18) and understanding (p. 107). Students may not realize that on p. 83, Collins is using Katniss's self-answered questions to steer reader understanding and expectation away from the truth [see Strategy 19 for more on this].
3. The Choice Analysis Tool shows us that Katniss's choice was terrorized—voluntary under the circumstances, but in a situation in which she faced her own and Peeta's death, inability to live with herself (*HG*, p. 343), and shame at home (*HG*, p. 247). The good she is seeking is life itself, both for herself and for Peeta. She has only partial information: she knows the tools she has available—her bow and arrow, the berries—but she can only guess about the Gamemakers' response to anything she might do. The choice is final—if

she's wrong, she'll be dead within seconds. In evaluating her comments, the Tool (and common sense) show that Katniss's choice to define her identity based on this single choice is ill-founded. Common sense tells us that our identity is not the product of a single choice in a single situation—our selves are the products of a lifetime of choices, however long or short that life is. Being human, we will make mistakes and do things we are less proud of, but these do not completely define us, provided we have done other things as well. The Choice Analysis Tool—by showing us what kind of choice this was—gives further reason to find Katniss's using this one choice to define herself as problematic: she didn't have the leisure or the knowledge to couch her action as a revolutionary statement, and she should not judge herself based on that. Her comments on *HG* p. 358 give a more nuanced interpretation of her actions, suggesting a combination of motives that—along with saving both their lives—give a more realistic picture of what went into that choice than the single motive analysis in *CF*.

4. Amendment VI guarantees that "in all criminal prosecutions, the accused shall enjoy the right to a speedy and public trial, by an impartial jury of the State and district wherein the crime shall have been committed . . . and to have the Assistance of Counsel for his defence" and Amendment VIII guarantees that "cruel and unusual punishments" shall not be inflicted; but Gale was not afforded a trial or any defense, and punished with inordinate severity.
5. The line graph should show Katniss's emotional ups and downs in the chapter, aptly naming her emotions.

Writer's Forum 4, Analyzing to Discover Categories, page 42

1. a. In addition to 'appropriately apologetic,' students' categories for 'good behavior' might include 'merciful,' 'generous,' 'kind,' 'forgiving,' 'self-sacrificing,' 'grateful,' 'loving,' 'nurturing,' 'honest,' 'warm,' 'helpful,' 'noble.'
b. Students are likely to identify Prim as being merciful and nurturing (w/ Buttercup, Lady), brave and loving (at the reaping), encouraging (at the Justice Building), forgiving (of her mother's neglect). They are likely to identify Peeta as being brave, generous (especially with the bread in *HG* and the gift to the families of the District 11 tributes in *CF*), loving, kind, self-sacrificing, honest (*HG* allowing his tears to be seen, p. 48; telling what his mother said, p. 90), noble (hoping to die as himself, *HG* p. 141), appropriately apologetic (*CF* p. 51), etc. c.–e. Students should note the following techniques. Collins uses plenty of off-screen time for Prim, and to a certain extent for Peeta. She places both Prim and Peeta in desperate straits, so that the focus is on the danger to them rather than their virtues. And she makes use of Katniss's misunderstanding of Peeta to present the reader with a false impression of Peeta to counteract his virtues (*HG*) and the strain after their victory to avoid having his virtues as evident as they would be otherwise.

Chapter 9, Katniss Plans an Uprising; Second Trip to the Lake, pages 43–44

1. Possible response: Her categorization a) ignores the evidence for Peeta's revolutionary possibilities and b) ignores her own actual feelings for Peeta. Peeta's desire "to show the Capitol that they don't own" him (*HG* p. 142) and his suggestion that they might have been wrong "about trying to subdue things in the districts" (*CG* p. 81) show that Peeta is hardly "the Capitol's design," even though it would suit the Capitol for them to wed. And her desire to be held was a specific desire for Peeta, not Gale.
2. Although Katniss refers to Gale as her best friend, implies that he knows her better than anyone (pp. 4, 12, and 26), and says directly to Peeta that he doesn't know her (p. 103), of the two men, only Peeta sees the bigger picture and—contrary to what Katniss believes about Gale superior understanding her—has a good idea of how Katniss will choose (when she doesn't yet know herself).
3. Katniss can't tell how she feels about Gale kissing her, partly because her only comparison is kissing Peeta to try to stay alive in the Games. When she kissed Gale, he was unconscious (or at least, she hopes he was), and she pushes it aside to get on with planning a revolution.
4. On p. 27, Peeta says that nothing much will happen before the end of the blizzard and Katniss agrees, but this is a device to increase the characters' (and therefore the reader's) surprise at finding the dramatic changes in the town square.
5. Not only would there be a problem starting an uprising in District 12 because of the generalized fear, but also because of Katniss's limitations. Katniss could draw certain people and groups together, but she would need help with reading people, persuasion, organization, supplies, setting objectives, and communicating with other districts.
6. They both have been planning ahead to provide him with alcohol if his supply runs out (that Katniss was is already known from *CF* p. 10) and are concerned about his mental health and well-being.
7. Answers will vary. Students may think she's a disaffected District 12 Peacekeeper. Very astute students may predict that she's from District 8 where all fabrics, therefore (presumably) Peacekeeper uniforms are made. In any case, the wafer seems to be an easily destroyed symbol for identifying fellow revolutionaries, so she's probably trying to connect to other revolutionaries.

8. Students should mention the changes to the square (p. 128) and the destruction of the Hob (p. 129); the closing of the mines, failed tesserae deliveries, and food shortages; the cut wages and extended hours in the mines and the choice to send miners into locations known to be dangerous (p. 131); the intentional spoilage/destruction of Parcel Day food and frequent public punishments (p. 132).

Strategy 13, Understanding Parallels and Repetition, page 45

1. The passage in *HG* is factual background, while the passage in *CF* recaps and extends that background, with Madge holding the view that Katniss might have had in *HG*, and Katniss now recognizing the the mockingjay is a creature that the Capitol "never intended to exist."
2. Answers will vary. The similarity of size and protective feeling Katniss has towards both of them is understandable, but students may feel that Katniss calling Rue "Prim" and having Prim stand on her toes like Rue are stretches, taking the parallels too far.
3. Answers will vary. Students may think that it casts Peeta in the mold of "the guy who didn't get the girl," which helps make the question of who will get the girl more fraught, therefore more interesting. They may think that it's reasonable that father and son might have similar taste in women. It might lead students to wonder why Mr. Mellark then married a "witch" (*HG* p. 37) after having been in love with Katniss's mother.
4. The train trip in *HG* is to the Games; the trip in *CF* is the post-Games Victory Tour. In both cases, Katniss has to prepare to exert everything she can to stay alive—in the first case because she's a tribute, in the second because of President Snow's threat. These are her first two trips outside her own district in a country in which provincialism is enforced, so they provide her with an opportunity to expand her understanding and connections. The Victory Tour will build on relationships (Rue) and the personal following Katniss started to build in the Games, through being the "girl on fire" and her "trick" with the berries.
5. Peeta also begs Katniss to leave when she's returned to Glimmer to take the bow, after dropping the tracker jacker nest on the Career Pack. In that case, he knows that Cato is coming to kill her, and he is trying to protect her. In *CF*, he probably not only sees Gale, but the turkey, and knowing how Katniss feels about Gale, as well as realizing that the Peacekeepers know that Katniss hunts with Gale, may suspect that she will a) also be a target and b) do something rash if she sees, so again, he begs her to leave to protect her.
6. In *HG*, the inciting incident is Prim being reaped, which leads to Katniss volunteering and becoming a tribute in the Games, in which her life is on the line. But its arguable that the event that sets the action of *CF* in motion—its inciting incident—is Katniss's "trick" with the berries in *HG*. It is this that leads to President Snow's visit and mandate about how Katniss must behave (or, we must suppose, die, along with her family and friends) on the Victory Tour, so a parallel to the Games, played out in a different arena.
7. In *HG*, the reversal is Peeta's declaration of love, which changes the perception of Katniss and therefore her chances of winning. In *CF*, the reversal is the arrival in the woods outside of District 12 of a person who is using Katniss's district token from the Games presumably as an identification of a revolutionary intent. Peeta sharing his affection on national television, followed by the development of the love story (through Peeta's and Katniss's actions, Caesar's presentation, and the filmmakers' summary for the final Games recap) and Katniss's "trick" with the berries—which is read by some of the viewing public as a revolutionary act—has led to Katniss and her pin becoming the symbol of an incipient revolution. [Students may not understand this until they've read Chapter 10.] It suggests her influence will increase and suggests that there is a chance of the revolution growing and the ruling power in Panem being overthrown.

Test, Chapters 1–9, page 46

Vocabulary

1. These words have to do with Katniss's visit to the Hob, showing her changed role since her win and her concern for Haymitch..
2. These words have to do with the architecture of the Justice Building in District 11, where Katniss and Peeta go beyond their scripted speeches, Katniss is saluted, at least one person is killed by Peacekeepers, and Haymitch leads them to the (presumably safe) dome for a debriefing..
3. Katniss uses these words in her analysis of why Plutarch Heavensbee has a mockingjay on his watch.
4. These words have to do with the history of how the mockingjay came into being.
5. These words have to do with Katniss's and Gale's discussion at the house by the lake, during which she tells him about the uprising in District 8 and then tries to defuse his response, leaving him disgusted.
6. These words have to do with the supplies Mrs. Everdeen has available to treat Gale after he is whipped.
7. These words name some of the new structures in the square after Romulus Thread takes over as Head Peacekeeper.
8. These words are from Effie's complaint about her treatment at the District 11 Justice Building.

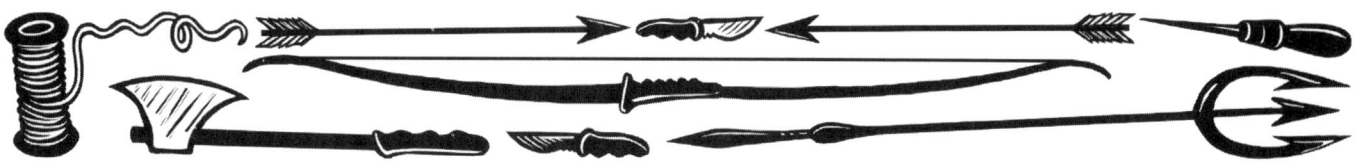

Essay Topics

1. The Victory Tour seems designed to keep the pain of the sacrifice of children in the Games fresh in everyone's mind and to promote disunity by confronting each district, and especially the families of the dead tributes from each district, with either their children's murderer or simply the tribute who survived when their own children did not. In every other year, with only one winner, the "celebration" could even cause disunity within the winning tribute's district, as well, since their other tribute died. That victors' children seem especially likely to get reaped means that even being a victor does not free a family from the Games. [Students may note that Katniss's comment about this (p. 45) is only treated theoretically—none of the victors Katniss meets in the rest of the trilogy is identified as being the child of a victor.] The Victor's Village in each district, the wealth of the victors, and the monthly Parcel Day, as well as the tesserae sign-ups and deliveries, also contribute to the fact that the Games never really ever go away.

2. Students are likely to say that the fact that many people in the district get involved in sponsoring tributes shows that they have a financial, as well as a regional and possibly a personal, stake in who wins, thus a greater emotional investment, which likely results in more animosity towards other districts when their own tributes are hurt, ensuring ongoing disunity.

3. Because her motivations were mixed—she says (*HG* p. 358) that she doesn't know what she did as "part of the games" and what she did "because I cared about him"—she's not sure if she should compare them with a kiss given purely with romantic feelings. Students may reference the kiss "that makes [her] want another" p. 298 as evidence that at least that kiss counted.

4. In *HG* (p. 9), Gale suggests that he and Katniss run off before the reaping. He then backpedals, referencing their family obligations. Later (*HG* p. 25), Katniss confirms that she was right not to run off, because no one else would have volunteered for Prim. In *CF*, after her visit with President Snow, Katniss considers that if Gale had no family, she would try to persuade him to run away (p. 33). She thinks of running away herself after Haymitch tells her that she'll have to marry Peeta, and she considers that any child she had would be likely to end up in the arena (p. 46), and puts the idea aside til after the Victory Tour. She proposes running away to Gale at the lake (p. 95), but he believes it's important to stay and fight. She also proposes it to Peeta (p. 102), and he says he'd go, but doesn't believe she'd leave. After Gale is whipped, Katniss gives up the idea of running away (p. 118–9) as a first step in what she'll do (p. 123).

5. Sound: chatter of woods; Touch: hot, muddy; Smell: blossoms, greenery; Sight: woods, small lake, blossoms, greenery, blue sky, waterfowl that nested around the shore, eggs in the grasses, shallows; Taste: dinner of roasted duck and baked katniss tubers with gravy.

6. In Panem, a talent is what victors give their time to since they are free from school and work. Evidence of the talent is both recorded (apparently for broadcast), and taken along on the Victory Tour train, although it's not clear what happens to it during the tour. It's also not clear what any other victor's talent is, besides Beetee and Wiress, who both invent things. Katniss's talent is meaningless, since it isn't hers.

7. Possible response: Haymitch must know that it's impossible, but thinks Katniss will be safer if she acts as if it is possible, so he acts as if it is and comforts her with the idea that marrying Peeta is not so bad.

8. Katniss's comments about Districts 3, 4, 8, and 11 indicate that citizens in those districts suffer more, leading to desperation and a strong desire for vengeance that don't exist in District 12. This suggests that President Snow is less worried about an uprising in District 12 than in trying to keep the Victory Tour tradition going while seeking to ensure through threats that Katniss will be focused on Peeta and convincing him (Snow) and not on the plight of the wider population or her potential power to move and unite them.

9. She's afraid that both they and many other people will be killed for a revolution that she doesn't imagine can be successful, having seen the Peacekeepers and situations in other districts.

10. Answers will vary. Students may suggest that the woman has come to spirit Katniss away from District 12, to get her to join in an uprising, to share news of the revolution from another district, to infiltrate the District 12 Peacekeepers, etc.

11. Possible responses: The person with the cracker will reveal herself and explain her mission and the significance of the mockingjay; Thread will target Katniss; there will be a confrontation between Gale and Peeta.

PART II THE QUELL—Chapter 10, Bonnie and Twill, pages 47–48

1. To be against the Capitol, which people assume Katniss is because of her "trick with the berries."

2. The first set was tracked and captured: the fact that this set doesn't think they were tracked and hasn't been captured may suggest a power shift toward the rebels. Also, Katniss has the power to and chooses to help this pair in various ways, whereas she did not help the girl who became an Avox (and possibly couldn't have). Bonnie and Twill were better (though not well) prepared for running away than the first set.

3. It reiterates for the reader that people in many districts (at least 12, 11, and 8) don't get enough to eat.

4. Answers will vary. Students may have observed that this is not the only time Katniss retells someone else's words, and they may suggest that Collins makes this choice to keep us focused on Katniss's voice, to feed us the information with Katniss's personal spin on it, and/or to save space. In this case, they may suggest that it allows for better presentation of Katniss's doubts about the existence of District 13 to have her retell their story.
5. In District 12, the Peacekeepers only (as far as we know) use tools for punishment of (purported) crimes—gallows, stocks, whipping post—and Thread is swayed by Purnia's mention of the code. In District 8, the Peacekeepers suppress an uprising using bombs, a lockdown, and televised footage of hanging of the suspected instigators, and then terrorist tactics, when they reopen the factory and set off a bomb in it.
6. She confirms that President Snow had tricked her and that "all the kisses and endearments in the world couldn't have derailed the momentum building up in District 8" (p. 149). But since she already had this realization on p. 71–2 ("No show of love, however believable, will turn this tide"), it seems like a narrative lapse to repeat it. The one difference is that she takes her analysis farther in Chapter 10, seeing that "it was a ploy to distract [her] and keep [her] from doing anything else inflammatory in the districts" (p. 150).
7. Katniss surmises that her wedding is another ploy to keep the Capitol residents entertained. This seems accurate, because it sustains the "love" explanation for Katniss's behavior in the arena (helping to quell the idea that it was rebellious) and also keeps people focused on romance rather than rebelling or shortages.
8. Some students may believe that it is part of the generally enhanced Peacekeeping activities in District 12 because none of the other changes seem particularly to do with Katniss. Other students may argue that it is primarily aimed at Katniss, both because she hunts and because she interfered in Gale's punishment. Others may say that both are likely true: it would have been done as a matter of course along with the other changes, but that doesn't mean that Thread isn't keen to catch Katniss breaking the law.
9. Answers will vary. Students may predict that her father left her a tool that will help enlarge the hole under the fence or figure that she'll find a tree with a branch extending over the fence to help her get back.
10. Students' summaries should end when Katniss leaves the women and not have any of Katniss's thoughts about what Bonnie and Twill said unless she voiced them.

Strategy 14, Understanding Shockers, page 49

1. Answers may vary. Possible responses: 2: President Snow shocks Katniss, and Collins intends to shock us, with both the fact that Snow knows about the kiss as well as the extent of his spy network that we infer from that. 3: Haymitch shocks Katniss, and Collins intends to shock us, with the understanding that Katniss has no choice but to marry Peeta. 4: Katniss is shocked, and Collins intends to shock us, with the death of the whistler. 5: All Katniss's over-the-top efforts and President Snow's appearance to congratulate Katniss and Peeta on their upcoming wedding will keep most readers focused on her quest. So the last sentence provides a cliffhanger as readers are left to wonder how President Snow will take his revenge. 6: Because of Katniss's comments on District 8 on p. 71, this ending is not as much of a shock, but it is a cliff-hanger—with a rebellion underway in one district, what next? 7: Collins gives so many clues that many readers will know before Katniss that Gale is being whipped, making this more of a cliffhanger (will Gale survive?). 8: Cliffhanger, leaving us wondering what Katniss will get up to in causing trouble in District 12. 9: Katniss and readers both meant to be shocked at a Peacekeeper who doesn't act like a Peacekeeper and has a mockingjay cracker. 10: Cliffhanger: how can Katniss get back inside the fence?

Chapter 11, The Electrified Fence; The Family Book, pages 50–51

1. First she diminishes her visibility, backing into the trees and covering her mouth to make her breath less noticeable. Second, she feels a surge of adrenaline, followed by a series of unanswerable questions about what the intention is behind turning on the fence. Next, she has a meta-moment in which she tells herself to stay calm and recalls other, similar incidents. She then considers her family's reaction—especially in light of her attempts to mislead them about her whereabouts—and her own concerns about whether she is being targeted, until she realizes that it doesn't matter: either way, she needs to get back into District 12 and act like she never left. She then begins practical steps geared to get her back to District 12.
2. A. If the electrifying of the fence is targeting someone, the list is pretty short, and includes her name, so for her own sake and her family's sake, she needs to get back to District 12. B. She has to get to the other side in a way that keeps her from touching any part of the fence. C. Burrowing under is not an option, both because she'll risk detection and the ground is frozen solid; this means she must go over. D. The tree she jumps from must have a branch strong enough to bear her weight and extending well over the fenceline.
3. She goes to the square and purchases bandages and candy. She greets her family "neutral[ly]." She lies about where she's been. She creates a fake argument with Prim about directions Prim supposedly gave.

4. Mrs. Everdeen says "brightly" that Katniss is "just in time for dinner" even though she's hours late. Haymitch asks where she's been in a "bored voice." Prim responds to Katniss's accusation of having given her wrong directions as if they're based on a convertation that actually took place. Peeta seconds Haymitch's recollection of the pretend conversation.
5. Students may suggest that the word was either *always* or *forever* because he's deeply in love with her.
6. Answers will vary. Students may suggest that President Snow would not be well-served by Thread quietly executing Katniss in the town square, preventing him from making a public and national example of her, so he might be in touch with Thread to limit what he does. Others may suggest that of course he is controlling everything. In either case, there's only indirect evidence on this point.
7. In *HG*, Katniss used the family book to help her feed her family when they were starving. It was connected to Peeta because it was in avoiding meeting his eyes that she saw the dandelion that reminded her that there was food she could gather, all carefully noted in this book. In *CF*, Peeta becomes more closely connected with the book, creating illustrations for it and doing something "normal" with Katniss for the first time. Since it is a "family book," some students may feel that this is a hint that her bond with Peeta is growing stronger, and they may consider it a portent that she will ultimately choose him, rather than Gale.
8. Katniss uses a metaphor of Peeta's hands, saying he makes pages "bloom"—that is, she identifies his hands with artistic ability and bringing things to life. She also uses a metaphor about Gale's hands (p. 27), saying that just as he could entrap game by building snares, he could "entrap" her. Considering what happens to the game that he traps, students may think that this is not necessarily a good thing. On p. 95, she reiterates Gale's ability with snares in noting the power and precision of his hands, but concludes by calling them "Hands I trust."
9. Convinced by the identical appearances of the mockingjay's wing that current news reports purporting to be from District 13 are mock-ups using old footage, Katniss is led to ask what's actually in District 13 now.
10. Students summaries should be limited to what Mrs. Everdeen observed/experienced.

Chapter 12, The Prep Team Arrives; The Quarter Quell Card, page 52

1. They reveal how dependent the Capitol is on production in the districts—possibly the way in which Panem is fragile that President Snow alluded to in Chapter 2.
2. Dough can take on many different forms and be used to create many different dishes: pies, pastries, dumplings, turnovers, pasta, as well as be altered with many different fillings, toppings, garnishes, etc. Katniss speaks about herself as if she were completely malleable and being given shape by her prep team.
3. The weather becomes less of a threat to existence; food is easier to grow, hunt, and gather..
4. Haymitch predicts that the Capitol may destroy another district as they did District 13, to make an example of it, and this does not seem unlikely, given its brutal tactics. [He proves to be correct because we hear the District 12 has been leveled in Chapter 27.].
5. If District 12 does not revolt, she is destined to marry Peeta.
6. The choice of the dress has been incorporated into an ongoing reality television show with viewers casting votes for their favorites and betting on the results.
7. The first Quarter Quell made citizens complicit in the deaths of their neighbors by making them vote. The second Quarter Quell killed twice as many, causing even more families pain. The third Quarter Quell reaps victors, who have already won the Games and were believed to be not only safe, but in positions of privilege for the rest of their lives, undermining the one "good" that results from the Games. The "usual" games predictably put all children age 12–18 (except those living in the Capitol) at risk every year.
8. Summaries should represent Prim's point of view and be limited to what she was present to observe and experience.

Strategy 15, Interpreting Intentional Contradictions, page 53

1. The use of old footage in news reports on District 13 is a clear case of the Capitol creating false impressions/lying, though what is actually there is still in doubt. The claim that they mined graphite may be an outright lie.
2. Answers will vary. Katniss says she wants to start an uprising (p. 127), presumably in District 12. Haymitch says it's not possible (p. 128), and given Katniss's observations, this seems to be true. But Haymitch does not address Katniss's clear ability to inspire the revolutionaries, evidenced by the Victory Tour and the cracker. Astute students may surmise that Haymitch is trying to prevent Katniss from doing something stupid or getting killed before he and his connections from across Panem (his ability to navigate the Justice Building in District 11 shows he has contacts outside District 12) can use her for a larger role (e.g., as the face of the revolution), so it is likely that he's trying to create a false impression.

Catching Fire: A Teaching Guide 103

Strategy 16, Considering Possible Consistency Issues, page 54

1. Answers will vary. At least some students are likely to view this as a mistake: given all the evidence of mandatory television watching for national events and everything surrounding the Games, and the intent to create terror through such announcements, it is unbelievable that watching the drawing of the card would not be required of all citizens. They may propose that Katniss's move to turn the TV off creates an emotional jolt from a state of being relieved because the show is over to being completely shocked at an unexpected and nearly unbelievable turn of events.

Chapter 13, Katniss and Haymitch Make a Deal; Training; Reaping , pages 55–56

1. She uses the drop cloth similarly to how she used the sheet of plastic in *HG* (p. 226) to keep warm. It symbolizes that she's already back in the Games.
2. Possible response: he is more emotionally honest, generous, kind, loyal, loving, trustworthy, and consistent than either Haymitch or Katniss.
3. Gale suggests running away to save Katniss. It shows a disregard for everything but her (e.g., the rest of their families), which might be taken as a sign of how much he loves her or how his love for her changes his goals or muddies his thinking, depending on one's perspective.
4. Students may think it shows that Collins doesn't trust her readers to draw these conclusions themselves. They may think Collins is correct due to the age range of her audience (younger readers wouldn't get it), or think she's misjudged her audience, or think it's evidence of poor writing, believing that if she had laid the groundwork properly, the meaning would be clear and not require overt explanation.
5. Mrs. Everdeen protects Katniss when she says Katniss is too young to date (p. 32), when she is the first to cover for Katniss upon her return after the fence is electrified (p. 154), and when she works to heals Katniss's injuries (Chapters 11, 12, and 13). She shows her abilitybto bear up under duress when she treats Gale's injuries and in her response to Katniss following the Quarter Quell announcement (pp. 180–181).
6. For the Quarter Quell, the waiting crowd has machine guns aimed at it, and the known female tribute and the two possible male tributes are already separated from their fellow citizens.
7. Although Katniss had chosen Gale and uprising rather than marry Peeta, she now has to give Gale up. The change in procedures prevents Katniss from having the goodbyes and closure she had counted on.
8. The announcement of the Quarter Quell card makes both Gale and Peeta think immediately of Katniss's safety. But it leaves Gale thinking that the only thing he can do for Katniss is leave with her, despite such a move dooming her family and his (and likely the two of them as well), while Peeta is put (again) in a situation in which sacrificing his life might save Katniss's, and he takes every step he can to make the odds for them as favorable as possible by enlisting Haymitch's promise and starting a strict training program.

Chapter 14, Other Victors; How Haymitch Won the Quell, pages 53–54

1. Katniss's attempt to make mental notes on the reapings has limited success, but she does recall: the beautiful siblings from District 1; Brutus, the 40-year-old volunteer from District 2; handsome Finnick from District 4, who won the Games at 14; the replacement of a young, hysterical woman from District 4 by an 80-year-old woman who needs a cane; Johanna Mason from District 7, who faked weakness to win; Cecelia, a mother; and Chaff, Haymitch's friend, from District 11.
2. Peeta stops being the hard-driving trainer and offers her comfort.
3. Possible response: amazing fighting and clever traps.
4. The attendant's behavior is the first sign of the Capitol citizens' feelings about the victors having to go back into the arena and is another occasion of Peeta's insight confronted with Katniss's lack of insight. Students may disagree about whether changing the apparent role/nature of the attendants was worth it and whether it just *seemed* that they all couldn't talk because none of them did.
5. Students may suggest she could have heard it during a photo shoot or think that it's so technical and out of her realm that its use is not believable. They may agree that if she was picking up video-editing terminology, more instances of it should be in the book. Students who believe that Collins did not stick to Katniss's diction and knowledge in *HG* may be more prepared to believe that this is a similar error. It functions to give readers the idea that the brutality of the Games extends to the filmography.
6. Students may not find it believable that Effie could get hold of a tape that has been banned from public showing. Even students who think she might may question Collins's failure to offer an explanation. The tape allows insights into Haymitch that would otherwise be unavailable.
7. They each repurposed a Gamemaker invention to win, and thereby made the Capitol/Gamemakers look stupid.

8. Why Haymitch's victory in the Second Quarter Quell was not discussed in detail in school in District 12.
9. Summaries should stick to what Haymitch witnessed/experienced.

Writer's Forum 5, Writing a Letter of Farewell, page 59

1. Answers will vary. Students should address the situation from Peeta's point of view and what they believe, given their understanding of him, he might have written under the circumstances.

Chapter 15, Meeting Victors and Chariot Ride; the New Avox, page 60

1. Peeta recognized the change in the train attendant's behavior, whereas it is only brought home to Katniss through her prep team.
2. Because Capitol citizens were not reaped, they never before had personal connections to the tributes prior to the Games. But now, some of their darlings have been reaped, and they are distraught.
3. In *HG*, she said, "I am not pretty. I am not beautiful. I am as radiant as the sun" (p. 121). In *CF*, she says, "I look as if I have been coated in glowing embers—no, that I *am* a glowing ember straight from our fireplace" (p. 206). In both cases, she uses negative constructions to build up from something lesser to a more dramatic figure of speech (simile/metaphor) to capture her stunning appearance.
4. Possible response: Katniss and Peeta would look weak and childish if they were chaperoned.
5. Since Gale did not die, it is hyperbolic, if not inaccurate, to speak of his life bleeding out, hence melodramatic, rather than simply dramatic.
6. Possible response: She will feel sad and feel that President Snow is targeting her in every possible way.
7. Summaries should only includes what Peeta witnessed/experienced.

Chapter 16, Making Allies/Friends; Time with the Gamemakers, page 61

1. It suggests that the red-headed girl Avox was also a plant, and that a) President Snow knew Katniss had seen the fleeing pair and b) the choice of Prim may have been planned to get Katniss into the arena, to silence her about the refugees and punish her and all who benefitted from her extra-District activities..
2. Students may see this as a continuity issue, since the concern seems to be erratic: heightened when it serves Collins's dramatic narrative purposes, and non-existent when it doesn't.
3. In Katniss's nightmare, she tries, like Tantalus, to drink from a pool that keeps receding (p. 221).
4. He doesn't want to give away to the other Gamemakers that he has any particular connection to Katniss.
5. She doesn't like or trust many of the tributes; she doesn't see how an alliance will help her save Peeta; as she gets to know the other tributes, the prospect of killing them becomes more and more troubling.
6. Possible response: Peeta painted something from the arena, and Katniss will get a very bad score.
7. Peeta, Brutus, and Chaff chuck spears; Finnick and Katniss tie knots; Katniss, Wiress, and Beetee try to light fires and discuss the force field around the Gamemakers; Peeta throws knives with an unidentified group; they all eat lunch together, and Peeta and Katniss sit with Chaff; Katniss, Cecelia, and Woof do edible insects; Cashmere, Gloss and Katniss make hammocks; Katniss and Enobaria do sword training; Finnick introduces Mags to Katniss at the fishing station; and almost everyone watches Katniss shoot.

Strategy 17, Identifying Tropes—Chekhov's Gun, page 63

1. Answers should include: Peeta's painting skills; Katniss's hunting skills; Katniss's reconstructed ear; Peeta's replacement leg; the force field with its "chink in the armor"; the nightlock berries; Rue's mockingjay song; Plutarch's watch; the pearl; Delly Cartwright and Johanna Mason (both mentioned in *HG*); Darius.

Chapter 17, The Tributes Take Charge of the Interviews, pages 64–65

1. Possible response: as a rebellious threat against their persons.
2. Possible response: treating the Gamemakers as criminals and/or murderers.
3. Haymitch is torn between his commitment and connection to Katniss and Peeta and to his longer friendships with other victors, and he expresses his frustration at their (foolish) stance through sarcasm.
4. All other things being equal, the other victors to target those who receive the top score.
5. She is quoting his words from *HG* (p. 142) to show him that she now understands what he meant.
6. An example of defiance of the Capitol, even in the face of death.
7. In the belief that she and Peeta cannot both survive, she considers his gift of words more valuable for transforming minds and hearts, and not having that gift, she thinks she is more valuable as a symbol.
8. Her private desire to keep Peeta alive and her public desire to defy the Capitol are in sync.
9. It recalls both their respite in the cave during the Games and the period during Katniss's recovery when they worked on the family book. Students may say that they show the possibility of / portend a normal life.

Catching Fire: A Teaching Guide

10. Possible response: Some feel that Katniss has upstaged them; some are actually angry with President Snow, not Katniss.
11. Summaries should reveal Cinna's view of the dress, which precedes Katniss's understanding of it.

Chapter 18, The Mockingjay Costume; Pregnancy; Attack on Cinna, page 66

1. Possible responses: They were jealous; they thought it focused too much on Katniss rather than the group; they weren't part of the "bomb building"; their anger was for President Snow for insisting Katniss wear her wedding gown, when she was not going to be married, but—most likely—would be killed in the Games.
2. Possible response: They have realized the horror of the Games for the first time; now the Capitol may face an outcry and loss of support even from its own citizens; the Games may fail as "bread and circuses."
3. In both cases, Peeta brings down the house, but in *HG*, he does it by speaking the truth, and in *CF*, he does it with a lie. In both cases the Capitol audience realizes how horrific the Games are in a way they never had before. In *CF*, most of the tributes (and in both cases, Cinna) have provided a build-up for him.
4. That in fighting to stay alive / save Peeta, she should not focus on her fellow tributes to the point that she forgets that the real enemy is outside the arena.
5. By Snow's threats, his (presumed) crafting of the Quarter Quell card; his making Darius an Avox; and his forcing Katniss and Peeta to dress as bride and groom for the interviews. By Thread in whipping Gale, turning on the electric fence and sending the Peacekeepers.
6. Students should choose appropriate moments and matching emotions.

Test, Chapters 10–18, page 67

Vocabulary
1. These words describe Bonnie.
2. These words are related to the uprising and response by Peacekeepers in District 8.
3. These words are related to the question of the truth about District 13.
4. These words are related to Katniss's successful attempt to reenter District 12 from the woods.
5. These words are part of Katniss's lie to the Peacekeepers about where she spent the day.
6. These words are related to the wedding dress photo shoot.
7. These words describe the deadly arena environment in the second Quarter Quell.
8. These words are related to Katniss's response to the appearance of Darius as an Avox attendant.
9. These words describe elements of Effie's plan of matching tokens for the District 12 team.
10. These words are from Katniss's interactions with victors from other districts in training.
11. These words are related to Katniss's dress for the pre-Games interviews.
12. These words are related to the the reaction to the interviews and the victors' show of unity.

Essay Topics
1. The level of critical detail varies, but the inclusion of Chekhov's Guns means that close reading is required.
2. Though both Finnick and Herrick express a *carpe diem* (seize the day) approach to life, Herrick's context is the natural aging process and passage of time, whereas Finnick's context is murder in the arena.
3. If the plan all along was to reap them for the Quell, then allowing them to develop friendships would add to the horror, hence, "entertainment" of that spectacle. But since they have power, allowing them to mingle and develop friendships at all seems to have been an either oversight by the Capitol, or a continuity error by Collins. That they are separated at some times, but not others, seems a pretty clear continuity error.
4. Eulogies should explain Cinna's role in building Katniss's "brand," addressing why he chose District 12, his particular feats of artistry, and his having Katniss and Peeta hold hands during the chariot ride.
5. District 12 clothing is simple, with a rented dress for the woman and non-mining clothes for the man, rather than an elaborate wedding dress and tuxedo of the Capitol. The wedding in District 12 is not an elaborate ceremony with the bride given away and a big party, but consists of filling out forms at the Justice Building, being assigned a house, and sharing food, when possible, followed by a song as the threshold is crossed, and the toasting.
6. Answers will vary, but students may either think it is clever or cheap.
7. Peeta's gift of 1/12 of the victor's winnings to the tribute families of District 11 (p. 59); victors being sent back into the arena (p. 175); the victors show of unity and Caesar's loss of control (pp. 257–8); the Capitol crowd's opposition to the Capitol's agenda (p. 259). These show growing unity in opposition to the Capitol.
8. The audience already feels emotionally invested in relationships with many victors, and particularly the star-crossed lovers from District 12. The victors exploit this, referencing their closeness. So the audience is already ill at ease and asking questions that they have never asked before. To have an unborn child in the arena, especially Katniss's child, is horrific, even to them.

PART III THE ENEMY—Chapter 19, Unexpected Alliance; Peeta Electrocuted, page 68

1. Students' arena depictions should accurately reflect attributes described in the book.
2. Katniss is surprised by Finnick's being an ally and by the victors killing each other so quickly. She is shocked by Peeta's death.
3. Students may suspect a rebel underground of which Haymitch and Finnick are members or at least an alliance that extends outside the arena, since the bangle is definitely from Haymitch.
4. He could be thinking that they should trust Haymitch's choice or be in negotiator mode or see no reason for confrontation at this point.
5. Following the first reversal / plot point, there is an increase in the intensity of conflicts that Katniss faces. Her influence is growing, and the attempts to stop her have gone beyond threats: turning on the electrified fence; sending the Peacekeepers to her house; and creating/choosing the Quarter Quell Card that puts her back in the arena. Having chosen no allies and being up against seasoned killers, it seems fairly certain that she will die until—thanks to Haymitch—it turns out that she does, in fact, have at least one very desirable ally: Finnick, and this is the second plot point/reversal. Students may note that the plot structure is quite a bit more difficult to figure out in *CF* than in *HG*.
6.

Choice	Type	Motivation	Information	Extent
Finnick kills District 5 drunk	terrorized choice	Protect Katniss, baby, self	? (it's not clear that this tribute's allegiances or intent at the moment were known)	Final
Other deaths at the cornucopia	terrorized choices	Life	?	Final
Peeta's choice to lead results in his 'death'	terrorized choice—free choice in context	Protect Katniss	Partial information—arenas are known to be deadly; he doesn't know about the chink to spot the force field [Students may wonder why didn't Katniss tell him about this]. He knows his information is incomplete.	Final (seemingly)

Chapter 20, Search for Water; Tree Rat and Spile; Tolling Bells, page 69

1. Answers will vary. Students may conclude that in trying to have Katniss both a) think Finnick is hurting Peeta and b) then be able to explain what he was doing, Collins has created an unbelievable situation.
2. The alliance functions really well, each person's talents and abilities contributing to a better situation for all (Finnick saves Peeta; Mags gives Katniss moss to wipe her nose; Finnick makes staff/cane for Mags/Peeta; Katniss leads the group and spies out the arena from above; Finnick and Mags make a shelter, and Mags makes bowls; Mags tests / Peeta prepares nuts; Katniss hunts a tree rat; Katniss recognizes the spile and how to use it and Peeta and Finnick set it up; Katniss rouses the others to get them out of the fog.
3. He makes a wry joke, relieving the tension a bit, and says he's okay, focusing on the others, not himself.
4. Answers will vary. Considering how much in love Katniss has been portrayed as being, he may be wondering why she's glaring at him when he's just saved Peeta's life.
5. She eventually recalls—after notable hesitation—both mouth-to-mouth resuscitation and the use of a spile.

Chapter 21, Fog and Monkeys; Death of Mags, page 70

1. She's showing less awareness of the audience and how she appears and no interest in winning sponsors. The only parachute so far has not been clearly for any particular tribute. She has referred to Haymitch much less frequently, only in determining that Finnick was to be trusted, in trying to show her desire for water, and in using what she knows of Haymitch to work on figuring out the function of the spile.
2. Finnick can only carry Mags or Peeta: she seems to be sacrificing herself so Finnick can save Peeta.
3. Possible response: Katniss has mentioned the rain starting and stopping—it seems like events may be timed and spatially limited by the Gamemakers.
4. The parallel is the chewed leaves that wick out the poison of the tracker jacker stings (*HG* pp. 200–201).
5. Saltwater barrier to reach the cornucopia; the stash by the cornucopia had nothing but weapons (i.e., no food); the deadly force field; finding water; the nerve agent fog; the attack monkeys.

Chapter 22, Johanna Joins Alliance with Beetee and Wiress, pages 71–72

1. Katniss volunteers for Prim; Peeta attempts to sacrifice himself for Katniss in *HG*, and they both are attempting to sacrifice themselves for each other in the Quell; Mags and the female victor from District 6 sacrifice themselves for Peeta; Johanna considers getting Beetee and Wiress for Katniss a sacrifice.

Catching Fire: A Teaching Guide 107

2. The whole dynamic is different: Her "request" is sassy and disrespectful, and though it is likely to amuse the audience, Katniss uncharacteristically doesn't comment on this. More notable is that the response is immediate, as if the gift was already prepared.
3. It suggests that outside the arena, they could be friends. Students may see a contrast with *HG*.
4. Students may suggest, based on her complaining cooperation, that Johanna thinks joining Katniss (hence Finnick) is her best shot at surviving, and therefore pays the "price" Haymitch said Katniss required.
5. The bells tolling 12; symmetrical lightning strikes at 12 a.m. and p.m.; pie-shaped wedges, with a plague in each (blood rain, nerve gas fog, monkeys, wave), and Wiress's words, "tick tock."
6. He does not mention Mags's death; he is probably still feeling too emotional to talk about it.
7. The four incidents are Finnick swimming to get Peeta and resuscitating him; Mags walking into the fog so Finnick could carry Peeta; the District 6 tribute taking the monkey attack to spare Peeta. They are each a terrorized choice (given Panem, arena); apparently free choice in that context. Given what Johanna said, it seems as if they may all have been part of the "price" of alliance with Katniss. That Finnick asked Katniss to cover him shows that he knew he'd be vulnerable as he swam to get Peeta; it doesn't seem that he even stopped to consider his own safety when he resuscitated Peeta, but they were both interim measures. Mags and the morphling seemed to know that they would die for their choices, which were pretty clearly final.
8. Answers will vary. Students' endings should settle issues raised by foreshadowing or open plot questions and be consistent with what has happened thus far.
9. Answers should include: *HG*; trying to persuade Haymitch of Katniss's talents so he'd help her win and helping focus positive attention on Katniss during his interview. *CF*: instigating donations to tributes' families in District 11 on the Victory Tour to help heal the pain of the Games; conversations with other victors in training to foster friendship; setting off "the bomb" in the interviews in discussing Katniss's pregnancy to convince the Capitol audience of the injustice of the Games; inserting himself between Katniss and Finnick (p. 277), defusing a potentially deadly engagement.

Chapter 23, Figuring Out the Clock; Spinning Island, page 73

1. While it might have ultimately been necessary to explain the clock to convince her allies, Katniss doesn't refer to need, but says "there's enough time" to explain it (p. 325). Given her explicit concern with revealing knowledge of the arena (p. 284), Collins should have had Katnis at least explicitly considered the consequences of revealing the clock; that she didn't seems to be a continuity error (see p. 336 for her regrets).
2. Possible response: Katniss is wondering if Plutarch had known she'd be a tribute [he hadn't, p. 386].
3. "Hickory Dickory Dock." It seems like a lot of our current culture has been lost to the younger generations.
4. She fantasizes about killing President Snow.
5. He knows about the use of canaries in coal mines, though they are only in District 12.
6. Answers should reveal Finnick's point of view and only tell events/situations he witnessed.

Chapter 24, Jabberjay Attack; Peeta's Locket, page 74

1. In the wild, jabberyjays were used as recording devices to pick up citizens' conversations, and their "playback" mechanism was only used in the Capitol. Within the arena, they're playing back material that they've supposedly heard.
2. Possible response: If Katniss hadn't been there, that jabberjays were responsible might not have been figured out; a lone tribute might have gone insane.
3. She doesn't know how to refer to Finnick's and Annie's relationship, so she skips over the noun.
4. Answers may vary. Students may not be sure that Peeta believes what he says about the jabberjays; he is absolutely sincere about Katniss and her future.
5. Students should account for the confused/distraught feelings of the Capitol citizens after the interviews in their summaries.

Strategy 18, Assessing Various Types of Persuasion, page 75

1. She attempts to persuade: President Snow not to kill Gale (so far, so good); Gale to run away (failed); two Peacekeepers that she had not been outside District 12 (succeeded with one of the two); Haymitch that Peeta should be saved this time (in question); Peeta that she accepts his plans to save her (in question).
2. Sample answers (not all the examples are successful): appeal to reason—"They interview your family and friends. And can they do that if they've killed them all?" p. 346 *CF*; appeal to authority—"The required number of lashes has been dispensed" p. 108 *CF*; appeal to a principle, belief, or ideal that you and your audience share—"To show that I'm more than just a piece in their games?" p. 242 *CF*; using specific details—"I tell him about . . . President Snow's visit to my house, the murders in District 11 . . . the last-

108 Catching Fire: A Teaching Guide

ditch effort of the engagement...." p. 95 *CF*; appeal to force—"And then there's her family to think of. Her mother, her sister, and all those ... cousins." p. 20 *CF*; appeal to prejudices—"At least you two have decent manners." p. 44 *HG*; appeal to base instincts—"Go for a month, rewatch the Games, tour the catacombs. . . . " (indirect evidence) pp. 144–5 *HG*; appeal to emotions—". . . if it weren't for the baby." p. 256 *CF*; and charisma (since charisma doesn't need speech, this is an after effect quotation showing that charisma was at work)—"No one can help but admire your spirit." p. 121 *HG*.

Chapter 25, Beetee's Plan, pages 76–77

1. Students may think it reflects her deepening affection for Peeta.
2. All gifts have been for the team as a whole (or used by the team as a whole, even Finnick's loaf). Students should note the shift from a loaf of bread to rolls, and the repetitive nature of the roll gifts. Astute students, noting Katniss's complaint about needing salt, may think the number of rolls and district are a message, otherwise—given a gift of hot sauce—why wouldn't they send rolls from District 4?
3. At first, she considers Beetee's well-being, but she decides she must only think about keeping Peeta alive.
4. It could have been evidence of the Gamemakers choosing to save one or the other pack from death.
5. Peeta and Beetee both asks questions to bring their audience along with them. But Peeta appeals to things Katniss and Finnick both know from experience; whereas Beetee asks them to trust his ability to speak authoritatively about things they don't themselves understand.
6. Beetee's power has risen to the point that he's a de facto leader of the group; Katniss has become more sympathetic to and admiring of Johanna, but still doesn't trust her, and she feels more indebted to Finnick.
7. Answers will vary. Given that the real purpose was to blow a hole in the force field, students who know this and reason it out or who have studied electricity may doubt that it would have had the effects he claimed.
8. He realizes that he did not persuade Katniss with the locket.
9. She wraps up the pearl with the spile and medicine so that it will make it home with her and be returned to Peeta after she is dead.
10. Answers will vary, but students should mention: Who becomes the victor? Who is identified as "the enemy" What was Haymitch's plan behind giving Katniss and Peeta allies behind their backs? Was Peeta correcct that the tributes' families and friends are okay? Are any of the uprisings succeeding? How are Capitol citizens feeling about Panem's leadership? Whom did Haymitch really intend to save this time?

Writer's Forum 6, Writing Instructions or Directions, page 78

1. Students directions should include the information the Beetee shares on pp. 358–361 and 368–369, and they should flag the sections that aren't clear for any reason.
2. Students may say that Beetee's plan is not meant to be presented in an intelligible way. Answers may vary about why they think this is. Some may surmise that there's a secret alternative plan or motive and the stated plan is a ploy, meant to hide the real intent from fellow tributes, Gamemakers, or both.

Chapter 26, Johanna Attacks Katniss; Katniss Completes Beetee's Plan, page 79

1. Chapter 20, p. 283 when she says that from a sponsor's viewpoint, she's not handling things well, and p. 289 when she hopes a sympathetic sponsor will send her water; Chapter 24, p. 350 in reference to how interesting Peeta's remarks about Haymitch will be to Capitol viewers, and p. 353 when Peeta attempts to persuade her with the locket, but does not mention their baby until the discussion is almost over; Chapter 25 p. 361, where sponsors are mentioned as a potential source of food; and Chapter 26, p. 368 when she notes that the audience will be wanting more deaths, and may think that Beetee's trap will deliver them. With food, water, and allies, Katniss is not as reliant on sponsors; when she asks for something, the response is generally pretty immediate, and they get gifts of food even when they don't expect them.
2. Students may wonder how Katniss could possibly not notice how her arm was cut or that the tracker was gone while applying the moss to her arm and tying it on, or how Katniss could believe that, wanting to kill her, Johanna would just knock her out, cut her arm, smear her face with blood, and say "stay down," given Johanna's skill with weapons, her level of anger, and the fact that in that time, Johanna could have ensured she was dead. [Developments in Chapter 27 show that Collins's intent is to mislead Katniss and the reader and create a situation in which it is impossible for Katniss to get to Peeta or Peeta to be rescued.]
3. Answers will vary. Katniss surmises that he tried to drive the knife into the force field. Given his understanding of how it worked, he would know he would get shocked (and maybe killed), so it seems unlikely that he would do this (and fail), and it isn't explained. Students may also mention his similar arm wound.
4. President Snow / the Capitol. This is made clear by her descriptors: "Who starves and tortures and kills us in the arena. Who will soon kill everyone I love." (p. 378).

Catching Fire: A Teaching Guide 109

5. Answers will vary. Students may suggest that Katniss will be captured or rescued.
6. Answers will vary. Students may offer alternative answers to Katniss's for what Johanna did and what happened to Beetee [see answers to 2. and 3].

Chapter 27, Rescue of the Tributes: The Rebellion Begins, pages 81–82

1. Being picked up by the hovercraft: she never expected to leave the arena alive.
2. Possible responses: he intends to allow her to sleep; he hopes to pass her off as dead to journalists and then torture her for information; there doesn't seem to be a good reason for him to do so.
3. This is likely to speed the exposition and get back to the action.
4. 3: Wiress identified the clock and (by silence) an attack; Beetee created the means to blow a hole in the force field and stage managed; 4:Mags sacrificed herself for Peeta; Finnick got Peeta off the platform, resuscitatesd him, made him a cane, carried him out of the fog, and provided shelter, food, and guarding; 6: morphling took monkey attack for Peeta; 7: Johanna and Blight rescued Beetee and Wiress and Johanna brought them to Katniss, cut out her tracker, and led Brutus and Enobaria away; 8: we don't know what Cecilia and Woof did; 11: Chaff may have died fighting Brutus (p. 383); we don't know what Seeder did.
5. Like the Capitol, he has treated her as a pawn, manipulating her without her knowledge. Students may feel that the end justifies the means or that—given her insufficiencies as an actress—he had no choice.
6. Hating Peeta is her response to imagining that he may be happy in the belief that he saved her, which would be ironic because of her current situation.
7. She can't block him out; she interacts with him.
8. Answers will vary. Students may think that Gale would say Haymitch's deception was in a good cause.
9. Answers should be from Haymitch's viewpoint and include only what he knows or observes.
10. Students' artwork or titles should be representative of chapter content.

Strategy 19, Understanding Logical Fallacies and Narrative Misdirection, pages 83–84

1. a. Katniss ignores elements (fallacy of exclusion), like Plutarch's clear attempt to give her a hint about the arena when he says, "it starts at midnight" (p. 82), instead, casting him as just another spoiled Capitol resident (oversimplification). This creates dramatic irony for the astute reader and situational irony for Katniss when she finds Plutarch among her rescuers. b. Katniss ignores the fact that Johanna cuts her arm, not her throat, wipes her face with blood, rather than cutting her more, and says "stay down," when she could have killed her in less time (p. 371) and refuses to look at her arm, so the conclusion she draws suffers from excluded evidence. Students who find it unbelievable will find the chapter loaded with dramatic irony; students who believed Katniss's analysis won't.
2. Answers will vary depending on students' choice of characters for comparison. Possible choices include Professor Severus Snape in the Harry Potter series and Harvey Dent in *The Dark Knight*,

Strategy 20, Identifying Themes in a Series, page 85

1. Possible responses: *CF* repeats the themes of: Appearance vs. Reality (Plutarch Heavensbee, the arena, Katniss's 'capture'). It extrapolates the themes of: Food as Power in that food is not only daily survival, but the means of sending the message about the life-saving rescue; the Power of Partnerships by showing continued growth of interdistrict friendships and allegiances, despite the Capitol's efforts; Internal vs. External Identity in that Katniss is unable to accept her feelings for Peeta because she has branded him as "the Capitol's choice"—not hers. It personalizes the theme of Desensitization to and Through Violence by personifying it in Johanna. It deconstructs the theme of Bread and Circuses by showing the distress of the Capitol audience at the interviews, and pretty much removing the audience as a factor in Katniss's decisions in the games. The theme of Deception vs. Art is laid aside, for the moment.

Writer's Forum 10, Comparing Two Treatments, page 86

1. Students should address the questions given for guidance. Facts and opinions should be clearly stated and opinions should be supported by evidence. As in the first movie, the point of view is changed to third-person omniscient, and material is included both that Katniss was not party to and that is not in the books, notably, conversations between Plutarch Heavensbee and President Snow in which Plutarch is clearly using his influence to control what happens to Katniss. As with *The Hunger Games*, a number of changes take out problematic content from the books. Katniss does not irrationally try to keep Johanna out of the jabberjay quadrant after the jabberjays are gone, which Collins apparently did to reveal that Johanna has no one left that she loves, with that line made into a spontaneous admission from Johanna. Katniss does not draw untenable conclusions about Johanna's intentions after the removal of the tracker from her arm.

And Plutarch does not inexplicably close Katniss's eyes. Because Katnss's internal thoughts are not provided, the recollection of Haymitch's line ("Remember who the enemy is") is given to Finnick, whose wearing of Haymitch's bracelet links the two men. Also different is that Katniss comes face to face with Finnick just before exploding the force field and decides not to shoot him, while President Snow roots for her to betray her ally. Instead of the prep team, Effie Trinket undergoes the transformation from obliviousness about the effects of the Games to sympathy. In the movie, President Snow has a granddaughter who admires Katniss's love for Peeta and her courage and imitates her braid. It remains to be seen how this will be developed. The whipping scene develops differently and escalates more, with Thread first punching Katniss, then hitting her with the whip, and then pulling a gun on her, and being talked down by Haymitch, rather than another peacekeeper. Mrs. Everdeen is made weaker—she is unable to give Gale a shot of morphling because her hands are shaking too much, and Prim has to take over. Prim's role is expanded in other ways, as well, chiefly when she tells Katniss that she senses a change in the community in a growing feeling of hope. Also, Katniss sees Peeta's image of Rue for the Gamemakers (presumably so we can), and Plutarch does not give hints about the arena during his dance with Katniss. Madge is absent, the scenes of District 8 are seen on the train, and the actors visages are not disfigured with scars and salve after the fog.
2. Students' essays should should consider the capabilities and limitations of each medium and the consistency and coherence of the works as they compare and contrast them.

Test, Chapters 19–27, page 87
Vocabulary
1. These words concern the anti-itch/sunscreen cream.
2. These words refer to the experience of being spun on the island, ending a fight and disorienting the allies.
3. These words are part of Peeta's attempt to convince Katniss to allow him to sacrifice himself so she can live happily ever after with Gale.
4. These words concern Beetee's wire.
5. These words have to do with Katniss's experience after being shocked and captured.

Essay Topics
1. Students should mention personal friendships, Mockingjay connections (Katniss as uprising inspiration to other districts), alliances (including the Career packs), and conspiracies.
2. Students should see that, although people are shaped somewhat by upbringing, they are also shaped by personality, voluntary-under-the-circumstances and involuntary choices, motivations/intentions/desires, information level and awareness, and emotions (see the Choice Analysis Tool pp. 20–21).
3. Responses should address: the fact that Haymitch didn't honor Katniss's desire for no allies (which probably saved her life); Peeta's revelation that Haymitch made promises to him as well; the fact that Haymitch had a plan in place to save Peeta at pretty much any cost and rescue both Katniss and Peeta.
4. Possible response: Since Katniss does absolutely nothing after Peeta leaves to contribute to Finnick's recovery, it is likely that Peeta's view of Katniss is overwhelmingly shaped by her saving his life in *HG*. From Collins's perspective, it's an excuse for him to go do the more dangerous task of tapping the tree, setting up the next rescue.
5. She wants honesty, Peeta, and the ability to make independent decisions about her life; she's been facing lies; Peeta's been captured; and her every move is under control.
6. The ending of *The Giver* is ambiguous: whatever Lowry may have intended, it is not clear to readers if Jonas and Gabriel die or live to join a loving community. At the end of *Lord of the Flies*, Ralph is saved from a manhunt only to enter a cruiser that "will presently be hunting its enemy in the same implacable way," as Golding says of the end of the book, so they are doomed. The end of *Catching Fire* is indeterminate because there is still another volume of the series to unfold, and the districts may still overthrow the Capitol.
7. Peeta lied about Katniss being pregnant and convinced everyone except Katniss, as far as we know.
8. The title refers to the spread of the "spark" Katniss started when she defied the Capitol to win the Games.
9. Ideas about justification will vary. Katniss as mockingjay is the symbol of the rebellion, thus what happens to her is critical not just to her as an individual, but to everyone in Panem.
10. Ideas about justification and evidence will vary. It's likely that Katniss's inability to dissemble means she would have given something away and doomed herself, fellow tributes, and the revolution.
11. Answers will vary, but students should mention that trust must be rebuilt between Katniss and Haymitch, and Katniss's mental health must be restored, which likely requires Peeta's rescue.
12. In *CF*, the parachutes are meant to communicate with others, not (except in the first instance) with Katniss, are pre-planned, and carry a coded meaning, with money, apparently, being no object.
13. The rescue of Beetee, Finnick, and Katniss is the reversal or plot point, dramatically increasing the rebels' chance of overthrowing the Capitol, although Katniss's mental health may continue to be a challenge.

THEME PAGES, pages 88–89

Odds and Chance
1. To send children to death while wishing them luck is hypocritical and horrific.
2. The more we learn, the less the odds seem to be involved: President Snow is "the decider" and the fortunes of outlaws and victors are at increased risk as the result of explict planning.

Debts and Owing
1. Katniss wants to repay her debts and owing someone trumps other considerations.
2. Lists should include Peeta, Gale, Haymitch, Rue, Thresh, Greasy Sae/the Hob/District 12 contributors, Finnick, Mags, District 6 Morphling, Johanna, Plutarch. They all contributed to saving her life.
3. In *HG*, Peeta; Katniss's thanks are often in her head. In *CF*, Katniss expresses thanks aloud more often. Peeta is more comfortable with a wide range of people and expressing emotions in general (he cries in public in *HG*). Katniss is a shy introvert, who is not very in touch with her own feelings and less adept at social interactions.
4. In a society in which districts and individuals are pitted against each other for survival, this seems true.

Appearance vs. Reality
1. Lists should include the aspects of false information from the Choice Analysis Tool: misinformation, lies, invalid conclusions, and wishful thinking.
2. Answers will vary, but students should include Haymitch, Johanna, and Finnick.
3. Capitol citizens' lives are built on altering appearances and the pretenses of entertainment.
4. They succeed in that they fool the Capitol, Katniss, and Peeta; it's not clear that the capture of some tributes was due to any failure on their part.
5. Cinna alters the bridal gown into a mockingjay dress without telling her. Students may say that Cinna is being treated as a martyr, with any questionable actions/choices deemphasized for the sake of that role.

Competition, Alliance, and Self-Interest
1. Personal qualities include belief in something greater than one's own life; kindness; love. Actions include sharing supplies, personal openness, covering for each other, risking one's life for the other, building trust.
2. Possible response: On sports (and other) teams, players have individual records and team records. In addition there may be regional, state, and national affiliations. So individuals contributions count for their own record and the efforts of the wider group.
3. It's not clear who would win in a battle between Finnick and Katniss, but their alliance is initially built on Finnick's agreement with Haymitch (to which we're not party) and Katniss's bowing to Haymitch's choice, but later to increasing trust, risking lives for each other, and Katniss's gratitude for Finnick saving Peeta.
4. In the arena, where one person's survival means another's death, neither of these quotations can hold true.

Abuse
1. Some analyses consider six types of abuse: physical, mental, emotional, sexual, verbal, and economic (http://www.projectpave.org/6-types-abuse); but there is also substance abuse. Thread physically abuses Gale; Snow mentally and emotionally abuses Katniss, Cray sexually abuses starving young women, Katniss verbally (and physically) abuses Haymitch; and Panem economically abuses its residents. Katniss and Haymitch abuse alcohol, the morphlings abuse drugs, and Capitol residents abuse food by binging and vomiting.
2. Haymitch turns to alcohol in the aftermath of the arena, mentoring, and having everyone he loved killed; Katniss does in anticipation of returning to the arena in the Quarter Quell. Panem doesn't provide many resources for more constructive ways of dealing with their situations.
3. He starts again as he watches the movie of his time in the arena on the train.
4. Possible response: It could be said that parents do not feed their children adequately, ensure that they have valuable schooling, or protect them from the arena. But the power to do these things has been taken from them, and it is the Capitol that is culpable.

Morality and Virtue
1. Students are likely to list many of the same qualities that they pointed to in Writer's Forum 4: mercy, generosity, kindness, forgiveness, self-sacrifice, gratitude, love, nurture, honesty, warmth, helpfulness; as well as bravery and trustworthiness.
2. She has promised to save Peeta, and plans to sacrifice her own life in the process. But she has a duty of gratitude to Finnick who has both saved Peeta repeatedly and contributed to her own safety and well-being. This isn't a choice between right and wrong: because they're in the arena, there's no good answer.
3. It's impossible to say that a set of religious principles is essential for the restoration of a national morality in Panem, but it's also unclear on what other basis a code of right behavior could be established.